COMFORT AND JOY

14 QUILTS FOR CHRISTMAS

MARY HICKEY

Martingale®
& COMPANY

CREDITS

President & CEO ❧ Tom Wierzbicki
Publisher ❧ Jane Hamada
Editorial Director ❧ Mary V. Green
Managing Editor ❧ Tina Cook
Developmental Editor ❧ Karen Costello Soltys
Technical Editor ❧ Nancy Mahoney
Copy Editor ❧ Liz McGehee
Design Director ❧ Stan Green
Illustrator ❧ Adrienne Smitke
Cover & Text Designer ❧ Shelly Garrison
Photographer ❧ Brent Kane

MISSION STATEMENT

Dedicated to providing quality products and service to inspire creativity.

Comfort and Joy: 14 Quilts for Christmas
© 2007 by Mary Hickey

That Patchwork Place® is an imprint of Martingale & Company®.

Martingale & Company
20205 144th Ave. NE
Woodinville, WA 98072-8478 USA
www.martingale-pub.com

Library of Congress Cataloging-in-Publication Data
Library of Congress Control Number: 2007007497

ISBN: 978-1-56477-763-8

DEDICATION

For thirty years I have been blessed by a group of friends called the "Sewing Circle." While most of us don't actually sew (we have a few exceptions), all of us participate in the best form of feminine support, love, and caring. It is to these cherished friends whose tenderness, love, and loyalty have sustained me, that this book is dedicated.

ACKNOWLEDGMENTS

Quilt books can only spring to life with the help of a team of people. This little quilt book is a record breaker for the number of people who assisted in its creation. As always, my husband, Phil, was a constant help and support at every step of the project. My friends Cleo Nollette and Dawn Kelly were incredibly stalwart in their assistance with quiltmaking, bindings, and exquisite machine quilting.

My friend Carolyn Eagan gave me a great idea by simply asking me to write this book.

Cleo Nollette, ever generous, made both "Watching for Santa" and "Danish Hearts" at breakneck speed, and then stitched bindings on seven of the quilts; Pam Cope stitched the beautiful "Christmas Star Wreath"; Joan Dawson built "Santa's Village"; Judy Pollard grew the "Little Forest"; Joyce Zivojnovich created the "Frolicking Frosties"; and Pat Blodgett helped me sew, sew, sew! Pat kept me company, kept me calm, told me stories, and offered her peaceful friendship.

It's hard not to gush and grovel over Dawn Kelly, whose kindness is comparable only to her giftedness as a machine quilter. She often gives up her free time to help me. She looks at the quilts, places them in her machine, and breathes life and energy into the designs.

A special thank-you goes to Moda Fabrics, whose lovely fabrics were used to create "Midnight Star."

The ever-kind, talented, and generous staff members at Martingale & Company continue to work their own magic on my bumbling words and halting instructions. They are consistently kind, professional, and helpful.

CONTENTS

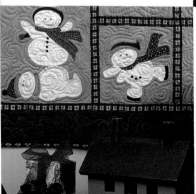

INTRODUCTION

This is a book of beautiful, straightforward Christmas quilts—nothing too complex or difficult. I've carefully chosen and polished the designs in this book to give them a down-to-earth spirit and a traditional flavor. At the same time, I've created designs that are exciting and dynamic, yet simple and straightforward. I tried to give each quilt a sense of originality and freshness that will spark your imagination and nudge you to try something new or perhaps a little bit quirky. The challenge of designing easy quilts is to avoid making them uninteresting or dull. The easiest way to do this is to use lots of different fabrics in your quilts. By using many shades of reds or greens, you can keep the pattern bold and strong, yet interesting and rich.

For some people, the word *Christmas* evokes visions of tiny children giggling, cinnamon smells wafting through the house, "Silent Night" playing softly, and glorious decorations warming the walls. For others, Christmas is the family gathering together in church. Whatever comes to mind for you, all Christmases share some basic characteristics: primarily a sense of coziness, a special feeling of family warmth and welcoming, and an air of joy.

Of course, for women, decorating the house is usually the first step in preparing for the Christmas season. No other type of Christmas decoration goes up so fast,

covers so much space so easily, lasts so long, or comes down and stores as quickly as a Christmas quilt. Christmas decor traditionally uses the lovely complementary color scheme of reds and greens, often with some tan or gold tossed in to convey a sense of warmth and celebration. The traditional color scheme can be adapted to any home anywhere. The scope of your decorating can be small or vast, depending on your sensibilities. This book focuses primarily on small wall hangings that can transform your spaces instantly to be ready for the season of celebration.

Some simple changes to the rooms in your home may be all you need to transform your space and give it the warmth and comfort of the Christmas season. With the bold red and green colors and their striking block patterns, Christmas quilts are a natural place to start decorating. The vivid patterns and soft, tactile fabrics of quilts can create an unpretentious Christmas style instantly.

The first part of the book provides complete directions for making a quilt. Next, you will find detailed instructions and illustrations to help you create your own little Christmas masterpiece. If you want a super-easy quilt, try "Watching for Santa" on page 88 or "Christmas Ski Trip" on page 104. "Peppermint Patties" on page 40 is also a bold but easy quilt. You can use your quilt to decorate your own home or to shower someone you love with a gift for the ages. Your little work of art can become an heirloom that will carry your Christmas spirit into the future.

TECHNIQUES FOR MAKING A
CHRISTMAS QUILT

Christmas quilts create a wonderful decoration for your walls or a coverlet for warmth. Most of the quilts in this book are designed as wall quilts and will be wonderful lifelong Christmas decorations. In this part of the book, I'll walk you through the process of making a quilt from start to finish.

CHOOSING FABRICS

Be sure to use only 100%-cotton fabrics for all quilts. Never start a quilt without prewashing all of the fabrics.

MARY'S HELPFUL HINT:
PREWASHING FABRICS

All fabrics destined for your sewing room must stop and visit the washing machine and dryer. Rich reds and deep greens are notorious for weeping dye into other parts of the quilt if they are not thoroughly prewashed. If any weeping is going to happen, you want it to be done by the fabric, not you! And, it should occur before the fabric is stitched into the quilt top. (This will prevent you from crying later.) Because you are working with 100%-cotton fabrics, the fabrics should be preshrunk and the excess dye must be washed out. Prewashing also removes the chemicals and sizing added to fabrics in the manufacturing process. Wash reds and greens separately in warm water in your washing machine. Check the water periodically to see if there is color flowing into the rinse water. If there is excess dye in the water, wash the fabric again. Tumble dry in a warm dryer. Remove and fold the fabrics as soon as they are dry.

For some people, choosing fabrics for a quilt is an easy Zenlike meditation process. For others, choosing fabrics for a quilt engenders a form of hysteria akin to mental breakdown. My goal in these next few paragraphs is to help you find a state of mind somewhere between these two extremes. In describing how I choose fabrics for a quilt, you may find something that will make the process easier for you.

Use different shades of red and green fabrics in your quilt.

Choosing fabrics for a Christmas quilt is exceptionally easy thanks to our fondness for the traditional holiday colors of red and green. Of course, there are many shades of red and green and you should feel free to consider any hue of red or green as a Christmas color. This still leaves us with the question of background colors. I usually let the intensity of the reds and greens dictate whether to use pure white, off-white, beige, or tan. If the reds and greens are pure and clear, use a white or an off-white. However, if the reds and greens have a lot of beige in them, use a beige, cream, or tan as the background.

Often a single gorgeous fabric inspires a quilt. This is the easiest way to pick fabrics for a quilt, because then all you have to do is match the other fabrics to the first one. When you see "Midnight Star" on page 83, you may think just a few colors in the gorgeous floral border inspired the rest of the quilt. While this is true, I used many different reds, creams, and greens in the blocks, giving the quilt more interest and visual texture, and making the assembly process more fun for me. Sometimes the quilt is for a specific person, and his or her decorating scheme gives me a sense of the type of quilt he or she might enjoy and tells me whether to use a warm, cozy Christmas palette or a clean, crisp group of holiday colors. If you start with at least one color or fabric, you can usually manage to keep going.

A multicolored theme or novelty fabric can give you a jump start for selecting the fabrics for your quilt. Look at the colors in the theme fabric and pick a few of those for the rest of the quilt. You can also choose one color in the theme fabric and use several shades of that color. This will keep your quilt interesting and fun to look at for a much longer time than if you just used one shade. Also, notice how often a color is used in a print and how large the areas of that color are. This is called color proportion and can be helpful in deciding how much of a color to use in a quilt.

I like to work in a style I call "controlled scrappy." This means I have a basic color scheme in mind, but I try to use several different fabrics within that color scheme. A good example of this is the quilt "Christmas Star Banner" on page 33. Although I've used a two-color scheme of burgundy and cream, when you look at the quilt, you'll see I've used more than just two fabrics; I've used lots of burgundy and cream fabrics.

Using several burgundy and cream fabrics keeps the quilt interesting.

Color Recipe

After you've chosen a group of fabrics, assign a position for each color family in the block. Place a different fabric from the assigned color family in the same position in each block. In other words, the colors stay in the same color family, but the intensity of the color and the print can change. By keeping the colors in the same positions but varying the fabrics, you add interest to the quilt without confusing the viewer. Be brave: vary the scale of your prints, use a variety of shades, and once in a while, do the unexpected.

Choose one color in the theme fabric and use several shades of that color.

CUTTING THE PIECES OF YOUR QUILT

Quiltmakers have devised a variety of clever strip-cutting and piecing techniques to use with rotary equipment. Who would ever guess that the "Christmas Weather Vane" blocks on page 28 would be made from long strips of fabric first sewn into a strip unit and then cut to make the little squares and rectangles? And who would guess that the stars in the "Midnight Star" quilt on page 83 would be made by folding squares rather than by cutting triangles? Yes, what we quilters really like is putting a little masterpiece on a wall or on a bed and having friends who visit think that we are quilting geniuses who spend thousands of hours slaving away out of love and devotion. Little do they know that we have been zooming along with our rotary cutters and strips, chatting and sewing and really enjoying ourselves.

Rotary Cutting

Good rotary-cutting equipment allows you to cut far more quickly and accurately. If you don't have rotary-cutting equipment, start by purchasing a cutter with a 2" blade. Check the instructions that come with it to learn the best way to hold it and how to use the safety guard. You'll also need a cutting mat on which to cut. An 18" x 24" mat is a good all-purpose size. Rotary-cutting rulers are ⅛" thick, enabling you to guide the rotary cutter next to it. The 6" x 24" ruler is most essential. I also find that a 6" Bias Square® ruler is indispensable. Note that rotary-cutting instructions are written for right-handers; reverse the instructions if you are left-handed.

Whether you are a beginner or an old pro, always follow a few precautions when rotary cutting. The rotary blade is extremely sharp, and before you notice, you can unintentionally cut a bite out of your good fabric or your finger. Make the following safety rules a habit.

- Always push the blade guard into place whenever you finish your cut. Keep the nut tight enough so that the guard won't slide back unintentionally.

- If you have small children (under age 20), keep your cutter in a safe place when not in use.

- Always roll the cutter away from you.

The Cleanup Cut

Cutting strips at an exact right angle to the folded edge of your fabric is the foundation for accuracy. Start with the first cut, known as the cleanup cut.

Fold your prewashed fabric in half with the selvages together and press. Place the fabric on your cutting mat with the folded edge closest to you. Align the fold with the horizontal lines on the cutting mat. Place a 6" x 24" ruler so that the raw edges of both layers of fabric are covered and the lines of your ruler match up with the vertical grid on your mat. Rolling the cutter away from you, cut along the right edge of the ruler, from the fold to the selvages. Remove the ruler and gently remove the waste strip.

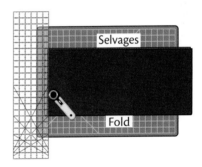

Cutting Strips

To cut strips, align the desired strip measurement on the ruler with the cut edge of the fabric. After cutting three or four strips, realign the fold of your fabric with the lines on your mat and make a new cleanup cut.

Note: All rotary-cutting measurements include ¼"-wide seam allowances.

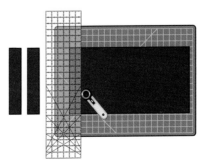

Cutting Squares and Rectangles

To cut squares and rectangles, cut strips in the desired widths. Cut the selvage ends off the strip. Align the required measurements on the ruler with the left edge of the strip and cut a square or rectangle. Continue cutting until you have the required number of pieces. Use your ruler and periodically check that your piece measurements are accurate.

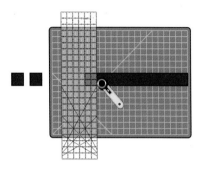

Cutting Special Motifs: "Fussy Cutting"

We're fortunate to live in an era when hundreds of adorable Christmas novelty or conversation prints are available. The "Watching for Santa" quilt on page 88 was designed specifically to use this type of print successfully. In most fabrics, the motifs are not evenly spaced, so you will need to selectively cut or "fussy cut" the motifs. A 6" or 12" square ruler is useful for fussy cutting. If you are cutting many squares, place masking tape on the ruler along the appropriate markings.

Move the marked ruler around the fabric to isolate a motif. Cut the first two sides. Next, turn the ruler around and align the desired markings with the just-cut edges. Cut the remaining two sides. If you have a limited amount of fabric, you might want to plan all your cuts first by using a pencil or a blue water-soluble pen to draw all the cutting lines.

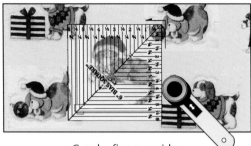

Cut the first two sides.

SEWING

The instructions and illustrations for each quilt project show you the steps in which to join the pieces of your block. In general, you will sew the shortest seams first and then sew progressively longer straight lines.

MARY'S HELPFUL HINT: RAPID RIPPING

I like to use this seam-ripping technique to correct a mismatched seam, because it's easy on my hands and the stitches quickly disappear. You will need a battery-operated mustache trimmer.

1. Start by removing the first three or four stitches with a seam ripper or a pin. Lay the seam on your right thigh.

2. Lift the top piece and insert the trimmer between the two pieces. Turn on the trimmer, and with a little downward pressure, *carefully* slide the trimmer forward, lifting the top piece as you go. The fabric on your leg and the downward pressure will hold the bottom piece in place while you gently lift the top piece. Use caution and practice a few times on some scraps before using this technique on your good fabric.

Blocks

Many wonderful quilt blocks are made up of squares. Often, if you had to cut out the individual squares and then sew each one to the next, the project would seem overwhelming. Strip sets are a quick and efficient way of cutting and piecing many blocks and block units.

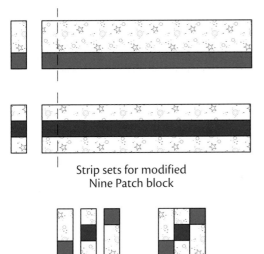

Strip sets for modified
Nine Patch block

After sewing strips together, do a cleanup cut to remove the selvage ends of the strip set. Align the required measurement on the ruler with the cleanly cut left edge of the strip sets, and cut the specified number of segments. Often, you will stitch the segments to other segments to make Four Patch or Nine Patch blocks.

Strip set for Four Patch block

Strip sets for Nine Patch block

Half-Square-Triangle Units

Several of the quilts in this book contain half-square-triangle units, also called triangle squares (see "Christmas Ski Trip" on page 104). I make these units the easy way, without cutting triangles. I also cut the squares slightly oversize to make them easy to sew; you can then trim and square them up after piecing.

1. Cut the squares 1" larger than the desired finished size of the half-square-triangle unit. The size to cut is given in each of the quilt cutting directions.

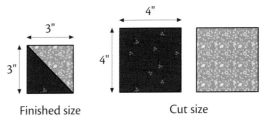

Finished size   Cut size

2. Layer the squares right sides together in pairs, with the lighter color on top of the darker color.

3. Using a pencil and a rotary-cutting ruler, draw a diagonal line from corner to corner on the wrong side of the lighter fabric. Sew ¼" from the drawn line on each side.

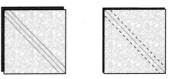

4. Cut on the drawn line with a rotary cutter and ruler.

5. Flip open the triangles, press the seam allowance toward the darker color, and trim away the little triangles or dog-ears that extend beyond the block at the corners. Trim and square up the block to the desired unfinished size. Each pair of squares will yield two half-square-triangle units.

MARY'S HELPFUL HINT: ASSEMBLY-LINE PREP

I like to stack up the squares and draw a faint diagonal pencil line on the wrong side of each light square while I sit and watch a good video or a baseball game. As I finish each square, I position it on the appropriate square so it is ready to stitch on the machine.

Hourglass Triangle Units

The following little trick with a half-square triangle is so clever I'm reluctant to mention it to nonquilters, because they'll find out we're not as brilliant as they thought. The "Christmas Star Wreath" quilt on page 45 features the hourglass unit.

1. Follow the steps in the preceding section for making half-square-triangle units.

2. Cut across the sewn half-square units on the diagonal to make two triangle units.

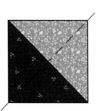

3. Arrange the triangles from two units as shown and stitch the hourglass units.

Folded Corners

One of the best tricks quiltmakers have at their disposal is what I call folded corners. It's another way of piecing triangles without actually cutting triangles and sewing on the bias. All you do is cut squares and stitch them to the corner of another patch, usually a square or a rectangle. Many of the quilts in this book feature blocks made just this way.

1. Cut squares the size specified in the cutting list. Draw a diagonal line from corner to corner on the wrong side of the squares as directed.

2. With right sides together, position the squares on the pieces as directed in the quilt instructions and sew on the drawn line.

3. Trim away the excess fabric, leaving a ¼" seam allowance. Flip up the triangle and press the seam allowance toward the darker color.

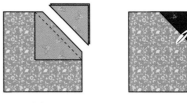

Trim.   Press.

MARY'S HELPFUL HINT: MAKING A MASKING-TAPE GUIDE

I like to place a masking-tape guide on my sewing machine to help me guide the folded-corner squares through the machine. Position the edge of a ruler directly in front of the needle, with the ruler extending from the needle to the front edge of your machine. Place a strip of masking tape (or use a permanent pen to draw a line) along the edge of the ruler. Be careful not to cover the feed dogs. As you sew, guide the corner of the square along the edge of the tape (or the line). You won't need to draw a diagonal line on the square.

APPLIQUÉ PRIMER

Appliqué involves turning under the edges of shapes and sewing them to a larger piece of fabric. Resourceful quilters have developed many clever methods to accomplish this time-honored quilt-making technique. The methods that follow are my favorites for the simple shapes used in this book.

Face-and-Turn Appliqué

1. Trace each appliqué shape onto template plastic, cardboard, or card stock and cut out each shape on the drawn line.

2. With right sides together, layer a piece of lightweight cotton or featherweight interfacing over the appliqué fabric for the backing, and pin the layers together. The backing should be about the same size as the appliqué fabric.

3. Place the template on the backing and trace around the shape with a blue water-soluble marking pen. Repeat to trace the desired number of shapes, leaving ½" between the shapes for a seam allowance.

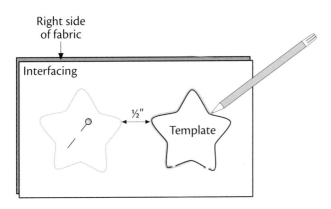

4. Using a matching thread and a very short stitch length, carefully machine stitch on the marked line around all the shapes.

5. Cut out all the shapes, leaving a scant ⅛" seam allowance. In the backing of each shape, make a slit that is big enough to turn the piece right side out.

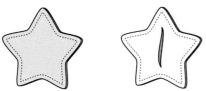

6. Using a spray bottle, spray the backing of each piece with water to remove the marked lines and to make it easier to smooth out the seams and points after the pieces are turned. Turn the pieces right side out and gently push out the curves and points with a knitting needle or chopstick. Press the appliqué pieces.

7. Since you've enclosed the unfinished edges of your appliqué pieces, you can simply bartack them onto your quilt, using a matching thread, or you can hand or machine appliqué them in place, using your favorite method.

Fusible Appliqué

Paper-backed fusible web makes quick work of making and applying appliqué shapes to your quilt top. I used fusible web to appliqué the shapes on "The Great Kindergarten Angel Christmas Pageant" quilt on page 72 and finished the edges with a straight stitch in a contrasting thread.

1. Trace each appliqué shape onto template plastic; label the front of each template. This is the right side.

2. Place each template on the paper side of the fusible web *right side down* and trace around it. Trace each shape the required number of times, leaving a small amount of space between the shapes. Cut out the shapes, leaving about a ¼" margin all around the outline.

3. Following the manufacturer's instructions for the fusible web, fuse each shape to the wrong side of the appropriate fabric. Cut out each shape on the drawn line.

4. Remove the paper and position the shape on the background fabric. Fuse the appliqué pieces in place.

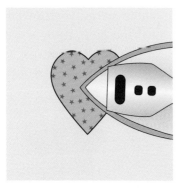

5. Using a matching or contrasting thread and a straight, zigzag, or blanket stitch, machine stitch around the outside of each shape.

MARY'S HELPFUL HINT: CHOOSING A FUSIBLE WEB

If you plan to sew a hand buttonhole stitch around your fused appliqué shapes, use a sheer to lightweight fusible web. If you don't plan to stitch through the shape, use a heavy-weight fusible web, but be aware that the additional bonding agent can make the fused area stiff and difficult to stitch through.

SQUARING UP THE BLOCKS

Once you've completed the blocks for your quilt, it's time to measure them. Measure all the blocks for your quilt; if the difference between the blocks is more than $\frac{1}{16}$", you'll need to trim all the blocks to the smallest size. Keep in mind that if you reduce the size of your blocks, you must also reduce the size of any related pieces that make up the quilt top, such as sashing or setting blocks.

1. Mark the size of the smallest block on a square ruler by placing a piece of masking tape along the horizontal and vertical measurements. In this example, we have marked the ruler at the 6¼" marking so we can trim the blocks to that size. Mark the ruler with a dot of tape at the center of the block measurement. In this example, half of 6¼" would be 3⅛"; therefore, 3⅛" would be the center of your block. Insert a small pin through the center of the block.

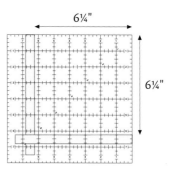

2. Align the center of the block measurement on the ruler with the center of the block and trim away the excess that extends beyond the top and right edges of the ruler. Rotate the block 180°, realign the center points, and trim the remaining two sides.

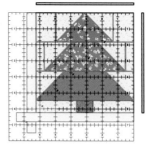
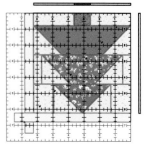

ADDING BORDERS

The borders must be cut to fit the center measurements of the quilt. If you cut them without measuring the quilt through the center, the borders might not fit properly and your quilt will end up looking wavy or puckered. Normal stretching during construction sometimes leaves the side edges of the quilt a little longer than the center, which is why it is important to measure through the quilt-top center.

The fabric requirements for the borders in this book are based on cutting the border strips on the crosswise grain, unless otherwise indicated. Cut strips the width indicated in the cutting instructions for your quilt. If the quilt is larger than the length of one strip, you will need to sew the strips together end to end with a straight or diagonal seam and then cut strips the exact length from the longer strip. Strips cut on the lengthwise grain (parallel to the selvage) will be cut longer than necessary and trimmed to size.

All the borders will be sewn to the quilt top in the following way:

1. Measure the length of the quilt top through the center. Cut two border strips to this measurement, piecing as necessary.

2. Mark the centers of the quilt-top sides and the border strips. Pin the borders to the sides of the quilt top, matching centers and ends. Ease or slightly stretch the quilt top to fit the border strip as necessary. Sew the side borders in place with a ¼"-wide seam and press the seams toward the border strips.

Measure top to bottom through the center.
Mark centers.

3. Measure the width of the quilt top from side to side through the center, including the side borders just added. Cut two border strips to this measurement, piecing as necessary. Mark the centers and then pin the border strips to the top and bottom edges of the quilt top, matching centers and ends. Sew the top and bottom borders in place with a ¼"-wide seam, easing as necessary, and press the seams toward the border strips.

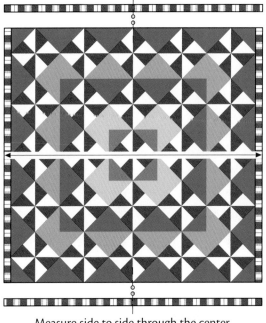

Measure side to side through the center.
Mark centers.

4. Repeat to add additional borders.

FINISHING YOUR QUILT

Your quilt top is now complete and you need to decide how you will quilt it. If the design needs to be marked on the quilt, marking should be done before layering the quilt with the backing and batting.

Backing

Your quilt back should be at least 2" to 3" larger than the quilt top on all sides. If your quilt is larger than the standard width of fabric, you will need to stitch two or more pieces of fabric together to make the backing. You can place the seams anywhere you want. Remove the selvages before sewing the pieces together. Press the seams open to make quilting the top easier.

Layering and Basting

Open and unroll the batting and allow it to "relax" overnight. Press the backing fabric and quilt top. Spread the backing, wrong side up, on a clean, flat surface. Use masking tape to anchor the backing to the surface without stretching the fabric. Spread the quilt batting on the backing, making sure it covers the entire backing and is smooth. Center the pressed and marked top, right side up, on the batting and backing. Align borders and straight lines of the quilt top with the edges of the backing. Pin the layers together along the edges with large straight pins to hold the layers smooth.

For machine quilting, use 1" rustproof safety pins to baste the layers together. Insert the pins as you would straight pins; start pinning in the center and work toward the outer edges of the quilt. Place the pins about 4" to 6" apart; try to avoid pinning over areas where you intend to quilt. Remove the large straight pins and use

a needle and thread to baste a line of stitches around the outside edges. This will keep the edges from raveling while you quilt and the edges aligned when you stitch the binding to the quilt. Remove the layered quilt from the hard surface; check the back to be sure it's smooth and close the safety pins.

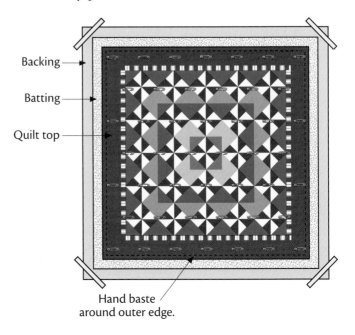

Hand baste around outer edge.

For hand quilting, it's best to thread baste the quilt; safety pins will get in the way of hoops or frames. Use a long needle and light-colored thread. If you thread your needle without cutting the thread off the spool, you will be able to baste at least two rows without rethreading your needle. Start at the center of the quilt and use large running stitches to baste across the quilt from side to side and top to bottom. Continue basting, creating a grid of parallel lines 6" to 8" apart. Complete the basting with a line of stitches around the outside edges to prevent the edges from raveling while you quilt and to keep the edges aligned when you are binding the quilt. After the basting is complete, remove all pins and masking tape.

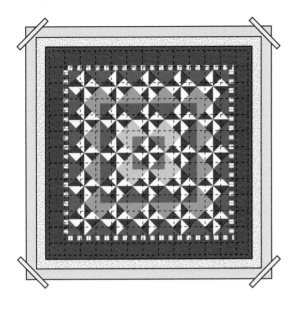

Quilting

It's a personal choice as to whether you want to hand or machine quilt your quilts. For some quilters, the most enjoyable part of making a quilt is the hand quilting. It's relaxing to sit and stitch while visiting with friends or riding in the car. Machine quilting should not be ignored, however. While machine quilting is faster than hand quilting, it is still an art that requires creativity and skill. Practice will make it fun and easy. The effort is well worth it, as you can complete a Christmas quilt in a single night.

There are many excellent books available to guide you through hand and machine quilting; I urge you to consult one if you need more information.

When all the quilting is completed, leave the basting stitches around the edges intact and remove the remaining basting stitches or pins. Trim the batting and backing even with the quilt top. Make sure the corners are square. What a wonderful moment this is!

Making a Hanging Sleeve

If you are going to hang your quilt, attach a sleeve or rod pocket to the back before you bind the quilt.

1. From the leftover backing fabric, cut a strip the width of your quilt by 8". On each end, fold under a ½" hem and then fold under ½" again; press and stitch.

2. Fold the strip in half lengthwise, wrong sides together. Stitch ¼" from the raw edges to make a tube; press. With the raw edges aligned, center the tube along the top edge of the quilt back. Baste it in place. Slip-stitch the bottom edge of the sleeve to the backing fabric. When you machine stitch the binding in place, you will also stitch the sleeve to the top, hiding the raw edges in the binding.

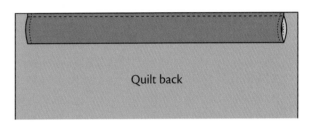

Quilt back

Binding Your Quilt

I like to make double-fold binding cut from straight-grain strips as this is the easiest binding to make and stitch. However, if you have a fabric with a directional design, such as a stripe or plaid, cut your strips on the bias to achieve the desired look. You will need to cut enough strips to go around the perimeter of the quilt plus 12" extra for seams and the corners in a mitered fold. Cut 2½"-wide strips across the width of the fabric as required for your quilt.

1. Join the strips at right angles and stitch across the corner as shown. Trim the excess fabric and press the seams open.

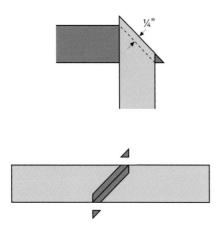

2. Fold the binding in half lengthwise, wrong sides together, and press.

3. Beginning at about the center of one side, align the raw edges of the folded binding with the edge of the quilt-top front. Leaving the first 10" unstitched, stitch the binding, using a ¼"-wide seam.

4. Stop stitching ¼" from the corner; backstitch. Remove the quilt from the sewing machine.

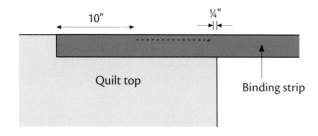

10"

¼"

Quilt top

Binding strip

5. Fold the binding up, away from the quilt, so the fold forms a 45° angle; then fold the binding back down so it is even with the next side as shown. Begin stitching at the edge of the binding and continue until you are ¼" from the next corner. Repeat this process at each corner.

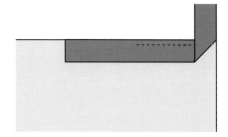

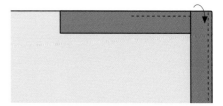

6. Stop stitching 10" from where you started. Remove the quilt from the machine and lay it on a flat surface. Fold the unstitched binding ends back on themselves so the folds just meet in the middle over the unsewn area of the quilt edge. Press the folds.

7. Unfold both ends of the binding. Open and lay the ending strip right side up. Open and lay the beginning strip over it, right side down, matching the centers of the pressed Xs. Carefully draw a diagonal line through the point where the fold lines meet. Pin and then stitch on the marked line. Check to make sure the newly sewn binding fits the unbound edge. Trim off the tail ends ¼" from the sewn seam; press the seam open.

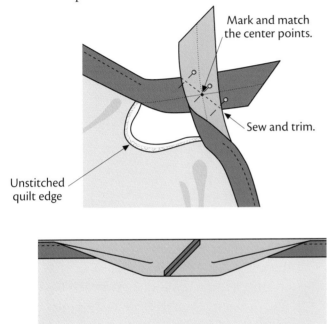

Mark and match the center points.

Sew and trim.

Unstitched quilt edge

8. Refold the binding, press the fold, and stitch the remainder of the binding to the quilt edge.

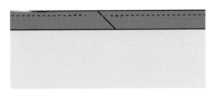

9. Fold the binding around to the back of the quilt and blindstitch it in place, using your machine stitching line as a guide and mitering the corners.

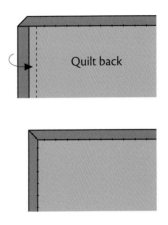

Quilt back

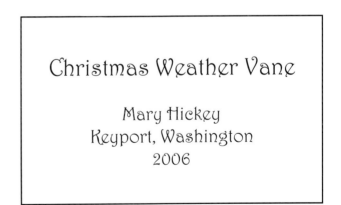

Adding a Quilt Label

Labeling your quilt is an important finishing touch. A label can be as simple or as elaborate as you wish. Use a plain fabric that coordinates with your backing fabric, and record the name of the quilt, your name, your city and state, the date, the person who is the recipient if it is a gift, and any other interesting or important information. This can be embroidered or written with a permanent pen or printed with your inkjet printer. If you are using a pen, iron freezer paper to the back of the fabric to stabilize it while writing.

Christmas Weather Vane

Mary Hickey
Keyport, Washington
2006

DANISH **HEARTS**

Few people celebrate Christmas with more exuberance than the Scandinavians. These joyful little hearts symbolize all the fun and joy the Danish bring to this festive season. I designed this sample using as many different reds and backgrounds as possible. This makes the quilt charming to look at and fun to piece.

MATERIALS

Yardage is based on 42"-wide fabric. Fat quarters measure 18" x 21".

1⅔ yards of dark green print for checked blocks, outer border, and binding

⅜ yard of green-and-white checked fabric for checked blocks

⅓ yard of white fabric for checked blocks

⅝ yard *total* of assorted red prints for Heart blocks; if using scraps, you'll need at least a 6" x 15" piece for each Heart block

7 fat quarters or 1¾ yards *total* of 7 assorted white-and-red prints for Heart blocks; if using scraps, you'll need at least a 9" x 18" piece for each Heart block

¼ yard of red print for inner border

3¼ yards of fabric for backing

52" x 52" piece of batting

CUTTING

All measurements include ¼"-wide seam allowances. Cut all strips across the width of fabric (selvage to selvage). Template D appears on page 27.

From *each* of the 7 assorted white-and-red prints, cut:

2 squares, 4½" x 4½"; cut once diagonally to yield 4 triangles and label them triangle C (28 triangles total; you'll have 2 extra)

1 square, 2½" x 2½"; cut once diagonally to yield 2 triangles and label them triangle A (14 triangles total; you'll have 1 extra)

2 squares, 2" x 2"; cut once diagonally to yield 4 triangles and label them triangle B (28 triangles total; you'll have 2 extra)

4 rectangles, 1½" x 7¾" (28 rectangles total; you'll have 2 extra)

4 rectangles, 1¼" x 8" (28 rectangles total; you'll have 2 extra)

4 rectangles, 1¼" x 6" (28 rectangles total; you'll have 2 extra)

From the assorted red prints, cut a *total* of:

26 rectangles, 1¼" x 8" (You'll need 2 matching rectangles for each block.)

26 pieces with template D

From the white fabric, cut:

6 strips, 1½" x 42"

From the dark green print, cut:

5 strips, 5¾" x 42"

6 strips, 2½" x 42"

6 strips, 1½" x 42"

From the green-and-white checked fabric, cut:

2 strips, 5½" x 42"; crosscut the strips into 12 squares, 5½" x 5½"

From the ¼ yard of red print, cut:

4 strips, 1½" x 42"

Danish Hearts, designed by Mary Hickey, 48" x 48".
Pieced by Cleo Nollette and machine quilted by Dawn Kelly.
Finished block: 7"

ASSEMBLING THE HEART BLOCKS

Each block is made using the pieces from one of the assorted white-and-red prints for the background and from one of the assorted red prints for the heart.

1. Arrange and stitch two 1¼" x 8" white-and-red rectangles and two 1¼" x 8" red strips together along the long edges as shown to make a strip set. Make 13. Crosscut each strip set into four 1¼"-wide segments (52 total).

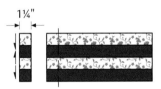

Make 13 strip sets.
Cut 4 segments from each (52 total).

2. Arrange and stitch four matching segments from step 1 together as shown to make a 16-patch unit; press. Make 13.

Make 13.

3. Using the same combination of fabrics that you used in step 2, arrange and sew one A triangle, two B triangles, two red D pieces, and one 16-patch unit as shown; press. Make 13. *Note that pieces D and Dr are not symmetrical. Be careful to arrange and sew A and B triangles to the correct sides of pieces D and Dr as shown.*

4. Stitch two C triangles to a heart unit from step 3; press. Trim the background pieces even with the edges of the red D pieces. Be sure to leave a ¼" seam allowance beyond the crossed seams at the base of the heart. Make 13.

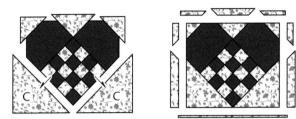

Make 13.

5. Sew a 1¼" x 6" white-and-red rectangle to opposite sides of the heart unit; press. Then sew a 1½" x 7¾" strip to the top and bottom; press. Refer to "Squaring Up the Blocks" on page 16 and trim the block to 7½" x 7½". Make 13 Heart blocks.

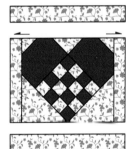

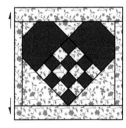

Make 13.

ASSEMBLING THE CHECKED BLOCKS

1. Arrange and stitch three 1½" x 42" white strips and two 1½" x 42" dark green strips together as shown to make strip set A. Press as shown. Crosscut the strip set into 24 segments, 1½" wide.

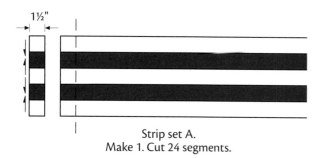

1½"

Strip set A.
Make 1. Cut 24 segments.

2. Arrange and stitch the remaining four 1½" x 42" dark green strips and three 1½" x 42" white strips together as shown to make strip set B. Press as shown. Crosscut the strip set into 24 segments, 1½" wide.

1½"

Strip set B.
Make 1. Cut 24 segments.

3. Stitch a 5½" green-and-white checked square between two segments from strip set A as shown; press.

4. Sew a segment from strip set B to the top and bottom of the unit to complete one block; press. Make 12 checked blocks.

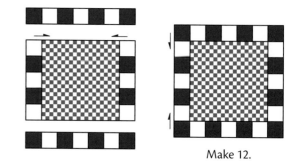

Make 12.

ASSEMBLING THE QUILT TOP

1. Refer to the assembly diagram on page 27 to arrange the blocks in five rows of five blocks each, alternating the Heart blocks and the checked blocks in each row and from row to row as shown.

2. Sew the blocks together in rows, pressing the seams toward the checked blocks. Sew the rows together, pressing the seam allowances in one direction.

3. Refer to "Adding Borders" on page 17. Measure, cut, and sew the 1½"-wide red inner-border strips and then the 5¾"-wide dark green outer-border strips to the quilt top.

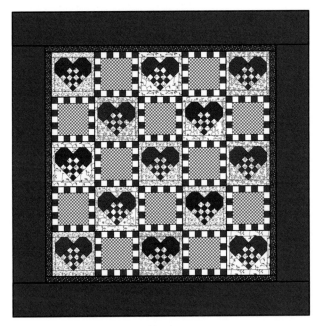

Assembly diagram

FINISHING THE QUILT

For detailed instructions on the following finishing techniques, refer to "Finishing Your Quilt" on page 18.

1. Cut and piece the backing fabric so that it is approximately 4" to 6" larger than the quilt top. Layer the quilt top with batting and backing. Baste the layers together.

2. Hand or machine quilt as desired. The quilt shown was machine quilted with a graceful heart medallion in the Heart blocks and curving crosses, straight crosses, and in-the-ditch quilting in the checked blocks. The borders have a vine design with heart-shaped leaves.

3. Trim the batting and backing fabric so the edges are even with the quilt top. Add a hanging sleeve if desired.

4. Use the 2½"-wide dark green strips to make the binding. Sew the binding to the quilt. Add a label to the quilt back.

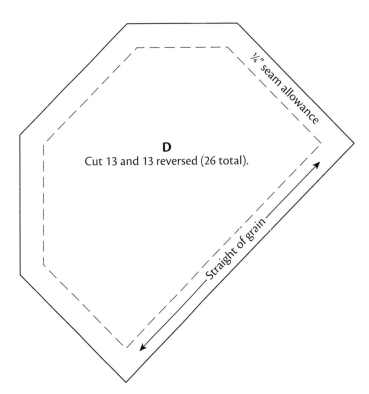

D
Cut 13 and 13 reversed (26 total).

¼" seam allowance

Straight of grain

CHRISTMAS **WEATHER VANE**

The simple Weather Vane block and Chain block make this an easy and dynamic quilt. The Weather Vane block employs a simple triangle method, and the Chain block uses the easy strip-set method for its nine-patch variation. The blocks combine to form layers of graphic design that look intricate but are really quite easy to make.

MATERIALS

Yardage is based on 42"-wide fabric.

1⅛ yards *total* of assorted white fabrics for block backgrounds

⅝ yard *total* of assorted green fabrics for Chain blocks, Weather Vane blocks, and inner border

½ yard of red-and-white dot fabric for outer border

½ yard of red-and-white checked fabric for Weather Vane blocks and binding

¼ yard of dark red fabric for Weather Vane blocks

2⅜ yards of fabric for backing*

43" x 43" piece of batting

*If backing fabric is 42" wide after washing, you can use a single width of 1⅜ yards.

CUTTING

All measurements include ¼"-wide seam allowances. Cut all strips across the width of fabric (selvage to selvage).

From the assorted white fabrics, cut a *total* of:
2 strips, 4½" x 42"; crosscut into 2 rectangles, 4½" x 15," and 8 rectangles, 2½" x 4½"

2 strips, 4¼" x 42"; crosscut into 2 rectangles, 4¼" x 20", and 10 rectangles, 3" x 4¼"

4 strips, 3" x 42"; crosscut *2 of the strips* into 16 squares, 3" x 3"

1 strip, 2½" x 42"; crosscut into 16 squares, 2½" x 2½"

2 strips, 1¾" x 42"

From the dark red fabric, cut:
2 strips, 3" x 42"; crosscut into 16 squares, 3" x 3"

From the red-and-white checked fabric, cut:
6 strips, 2½" x 42"; crosscut *1 of the strips* into 16 squares, 2½" x 2½"

From the assorted green fabrics, cut a *total* of:
3 strips, 1¾" x 42"

4 strips, 1½" x 42"

1 rectangle, 3" x 20"

1 rectangle, 2½" x 15"

From the red-and-white dot fabric, cut:
4 strips, 3½" x 42"

ASSEMBLING THE WEATHER VANE BLOCKS

1. Using a pencil and your rotary-cutting ruler, draw a diagonal line from corner to corner on the wrong side of each 3" white square. Place each marked square on a dark red square, right sides together. Stitch ¼" from both sides of the marked line. Cut the squares apart on the marked line. Press the seams toward the red. Make 32 half-square-triangle units. Trim the squares to 2½" x 2½".

Make 32.

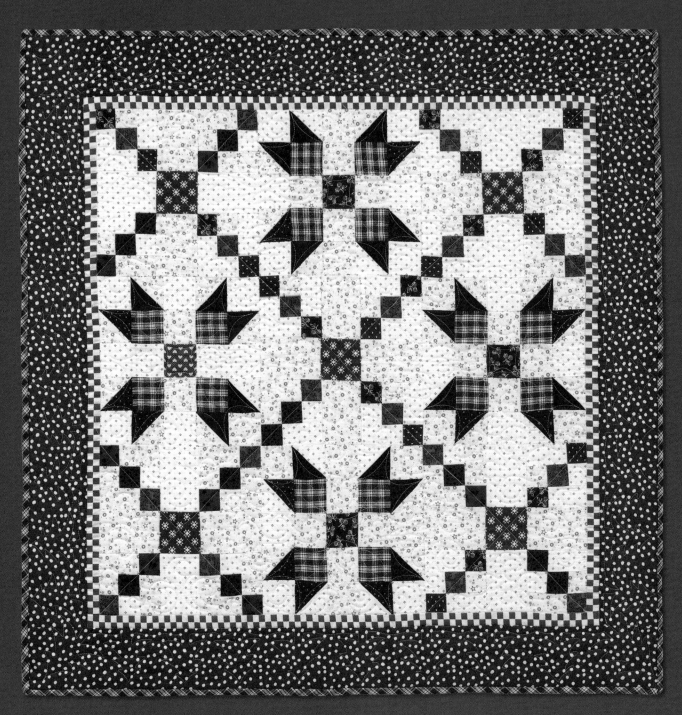

Christmas Weather Vane, designed and pieced by Mary Hickey, 38½" x 38½".
Machine quilted by Dawn Kelly.
Finished block: 10"

2. Arrange and sew two half-square-triangle units from step 1, one red-and-white check square, and one 2½" white square together as shown; press. Make 16.

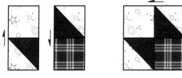

Make 16.

3. Stitch one 2½" x 15" green rectangle between two 4½" x 15" white rectangles to make a strip set as shown. Crosscut the strip set into four segments, 2½" wide.

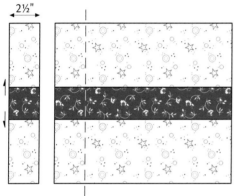

Make 1 strip set.
Cut 4 segments.

4. Arrange and sew four units from step 2, one segment from step 3, and two 2½" x 4½" white rectangles as shown; press. Make four Weather Vane blocks.

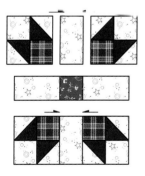

Make 4.

ASSEMBLING THE CHAIN BLOCKS

1. Stitch a 1¾" x 42" green strip to one long side of each 3" x 42" white strip to make a strip set; press. Make two. Crosscut the strip sets into 40 segments, 1¾" wide.

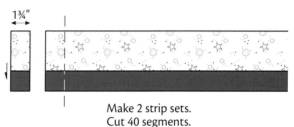

Make 2 strip sets.
Cut 40 segments.

2. Sew the remaining 1¾" x 42" green strip between two 1¾" x 42" white strips; press. Crosscut the strip set into 20 segments, 1¾" wide.

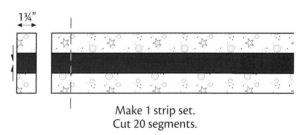

Make 1 strip set.
Cut 20 segments.

3. Sew one segment from step 2 between two segments from step 1 as shown; press. Make 20 units.

Make 20.

4. Sew the 3" x 20" green rectangle between two 4¼" x 20" white rectangles to make a strip set; press. Crosscut the strip set into five segments, 3" wide.

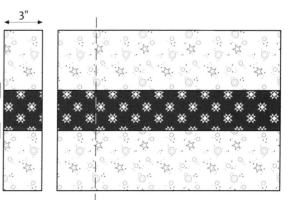

Make 1 strip set.
Cut 5 segments.

5. Stitch four units from step 3, one segment from step 4, and two 3" x 4¼" white rectangles together as shown; press. Make five Chain blocks.

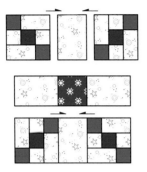
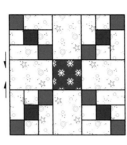

Make 5.

ASSEMBLING THE QUILT TOP

1. Refer to the assembly diagram to arrange the blocks in three rows of three blocks each, alternating the Weather Vane blocks and Chain blocks in each row and from row to row as shown.

2. Stitch the blocks together in rows; press toward the Chain blocks. Sew the rows together, pressing the seam allowances in one direction.

3. Refer to "Adding Borders" on page 17. Measure, cut, and sew the 1½"-wide green inner-border strips and then the 3½"-wide red-and-white dot outer-border strips to the quilt top.

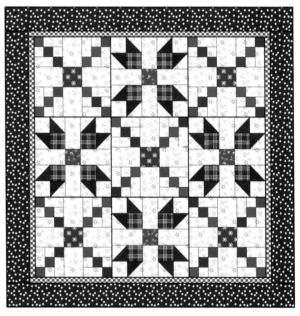

Assembly diagram

FINISHING THE QUILT

For detailed instructions on the following finishing techniques, refer to "Finishing Your Quilt" on page 18.

1. Cut and piece the backing fabric so that it is approximately 4" to 6" larger than the quilt top. Layer the quilt top with batting and backing. Baste the layers together.

2. Hand or machine quilt as desired. The quilt shown was machine quilted with arcs in the block swirls in the background and a jaunty tree design in the borders.

3. Trim the batting and backing fabric so the edges are even with the quilt top. Add a hanging sleeve if desired.

4. Use the 2½"-wide red-and-white check strips to make the binding. Sew the binding to the quilt. Add a label to the quilt back.

CHRISTMAS STAR **BANNER**

The stars in this quilt are easy and fun to make using the folded-corner method. The five stars with the adorable smaller stars inside them are just enough to add great interest to the quilt without significantly increasing the difficulty. And what fun to take your rotary cutter and cut the bottom of the quilt into deep points. Simply sewing a facing to the points finishes them and creates a dramatic quilt. Using the tabs instead of a hanging sleeve creates a more contemporary look and adds excitement to this lovely quilt.

Christmas Star Banner, designed by Mary Hickey, 41½" x 58½" without tassels.
Pieced by Mary Hickey and Pat Blodgett, and machine quilted by Dawn Kelly.
Finished block: 8"

MATERIALS

Yardage is based on 42"-wide fabric.

2⅜ yards *total* of assorted burgundy fabrics for Star blocks, setting rectangles, top border, binding, and hanging tabs

1⅞ yards of cream-and-burgundy print for vertical sashing strips

1⅜ yards of burgundy facing fabric for top and bottom edges

⅞ yard *total* of assorted cream fabrics for Star blocks

2¾ yards of fabric for backing

46" x 63" piece of batting

3 burgundy tassels

Permanent marker

Knitting needle or chopstick (optional)

42"-long wooden dowel, ½" diameter, or metal curtain rod, ¾" diameter (optional)

CUTTING

All measurements include ¼"-wide seam allowances. Cut all strips across the width of fabric (selvage to selvage) unless instructed otherwise.

From the assorted burgundy fabrics, cut a *total* of:

2 strips, 8½" x 42"; crosscut into 2 rectangles, 8½" x 19½", and 1 rectangle, 8½" x 10½"

1 strip, 6" x 42"; crosscut into 9 rectangles, 4¼" x 6"

10 strips, 2½" x 42"; crosscut into 10 rectangles, 2½" x 8½", and 52 rectangles, 2½" x 4½"

6 strips, 2½" x 42"; crosscut into 89 squares, 2½" x 2½"

3 strips, 2½" x 42"

2 strips, 2¼" x 42"

2 strips, 1½" x 42"; crosscut into 40 squares, 1½" x 1½"

From the assorted cream prints, cut a *total* of:

1 strip, 4½" x 42"; crosscut into 8 squares, 4½" x 4½"

7 strips, 2½" x 42"; crosscut into 104 squares, 2½" x 2½"

3 strips, 1½" x 42"; crosscut into 20 rectangles, 1½" x 2½", and 20 squares, 1½" x 1½"

From the *lengthwise grain* of the cream-and-burgundy print, cut:

2 strips, 6½" x 60"

2 strips, 3" x 60"

From the *lengthwise grain* of the burgundy facing fabric, cut:

1 piece, 18" x 44"

1 strip, 3" x 44"

MAKING THE STAR BLOCKS

1. Using a pencil and your rotary-cutting ruler, draw a diagonal line from corner to corner on the wrong side of each 2½" cream square. Align a marked square on one end of each 2½" x 4½" burgundy rectangle, right sides together. Stitch on the marked line. Trim ¼" from the stitching line. Flip the cream triangle up and press the seam toward the rectangle. Repeat on the opposite end of the burgundy rectangle, positioning the marked square as shown. Make 52.

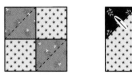

Make 52.

2. Draw a diagonal line from corner to corner on the wrong side of 32 of the 2½" burgundy squares. With right sides together, place two marked squares on opposite corners of each 4½" cream square as shown. Stitch on the marked lines. Trim ¼" from the stitching line. Flip the triangle up and press the seam toward the burgundy. Repeat on the opposite corners of each square as shown. Make eight.

Make 8.

3. Repeat step 1, drawing a diagonal line on the wrong side of each 1½" burgundy square. Align a marked square on one end of each 1½" x 2½" cream rectangle, right sides together. Stitch on the marked line; trim and press. Repeat on the opposite end of the cream rectangle, positioning the marked square as shown. Make 20.

Make 20.

4. To make the single Star blocks, arrange and sew four units from step 1, one unit from step 2, and four 2½" burgundy squares together as shown; press. Make eight Star blocks.

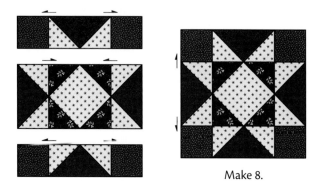

Make 8.

5. To make the center star for the Star-within-a-Star block, arrange and sew four units from step 3, one 2½" burgundy square, and four 1½" cream squares together as shown; press. Make five.

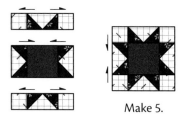

Make 5.

6. Arrange and sew four units from step 1, one unit from step 5, and four 2½" burgundy squares together as shown; press. Make five Star-within-a-Star blocks.

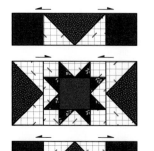 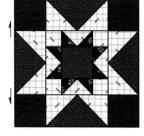

Make 5.

ASSEMBLING THE BANNER

1. Arrange and sew four blocks and three 2½" x 8½" burgundy rectangles to make a vertical row as shown; press. Repeat to make two vertical rows. Arrange and sew five blocks and four 2½" x 8½" burgundy rectangles to make one vertical row as shown; press.

Make 2.

Make 1.

2. Sew an 8½" x 19½" burgundy rectangle to one end of each four-block column as shown; press. Sew an 8½" x 10½" burgundy rectangle to one end of the five-block column as shown; press.

3. Measure the length of all three vertical rows. If they differ, estimate the average and consider this the length. Trim the 6½"-wide and 3"-wide cream-and-burgundy strips to fit that measurement.

4. Sew the block rows, the trimmed 6½"-wide strips, and the trimmed 3"-wide strips together as shown; press.

5. Refer to "Adding Borders" on page 17. Measure, cut, and sew the 2¼"-wide burgundy strips to the top of the quilt.

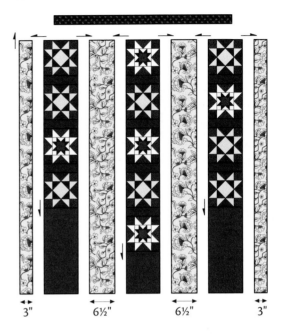

3"   6½"   6½"   3"

MAKING THE HANGING TABS

1. On each side of the 4¼" x 6" burgundy rectangles, fold under a 1" hem as shown. Press in place and, if desired, topstitch with matching thread. Fold the tabs in half. Make nine tabs.

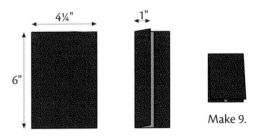

4¼"   1"

6"

Make 9.

2. On the front of the quilt, align the raw edges of the tabs with the top edge of the quilt top, making sure the tabs are spaced evenly. Pin and then sew the tabs, using a scant ¼"-wide seam.

CREATING THE POINTS

The deep points on the bottom of the quilt add a great deal of drama and interest and are actually quite easy to make.

1. Fold the quilt top in half lengthwise and lightly crease to mark the center at the bottom edge. Then use a permanent pen to mark a dot as shown. This will be dot A.

2. On the inner edge of each four-block row, measure down 5½" from the bottom of the Star block and place a dot as shown. These are B dots. Using a ruler and a permanent pen, draw a line from dot A to each B dot.

3. On each of the four-block rows, measure down 11" from the bottom of the Star block and place a dot in the center of the row as shown. These are C dots. Draw a line to connect each B and C dot.

4. For the last two dots, measure 9" up from dot C and across at a right angle to the outside edge of the quilt as shown, and place dot D. Draw a line to connect each C and D dot.

Note: The drawn lines are guides for where the quilting should end. If you plan to quilt the top by hand or machine, baste along the bottom edge; then cut away the excess fabric on the outside of the marked lines before basting the rest of the quilt top. If you plan to have the quilt top professionally machine quilted, don't cut off the excess fabric. The quilter will need the quilt top to be rectangular to attach it to the long-arm machine. After the quilting is complete, you can then trim along the lines.

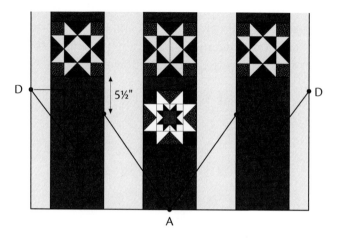

FINISHING THE BANNER

For detailed instructions on the following finishing techniques, refer to "Finishing Your Quilt" on page 18.

1. Cut and piece the backing fabric so that it is approximately 4" to 6" larger than the quilt top. Layer the quilt top with batting and backing. Baste the layers together.

2. Hand or machine quilt as desired. The quilt shown was machine quilted with outline quilting in the blocks, and poinsettias and an angel in the burgundy points.

3. Trim the batting and backing fabric so the edges are even with the quilt top.

4. Use the 2½"-wide burgundy strips to make the binding. Sew the binding to the side edges of the quilt.

5. Press a ½" hem along one long side of the 18" x 44" burgundy facing piece. With right sides together, position the facing strip across the bottom of the quilt front so it extends ¼" beyond the longest point as shown. Carefully

pin in place. Using a very small stitch and a ¼"-wide seam, sew the strip and the bottom edge of the quilt together as shown.

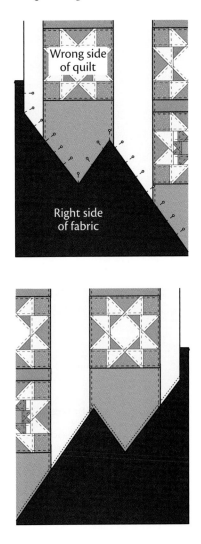

6. Trim the excess fabric ¼" from the stitching line. Fold the strip around to the back, and using a knitting needle or chopstick, smooth out the points on the bottom of the quilt. Gently press the bottom of the quilt. Along the side edges, turn the seam allowance of the facing strip under ¼" and pin to the back of the quilt. Hand stitch the top and side edges of the facing strip to the back of the quilt. Hand stitch a tassel to each point.

7. Stitch the 3" x 44" burgundy facing strip to the top edge of the quilt, enclosing the tabs. Along the long edge and both side edges, turn the seam allowance of the facing strip under ¼" and pin to the back of the quilt. Hand stitch the edges of the facing strip to the back of the quilt.

Assembly diagram

PEPPERMINT **PATTIES**

A variety of rich red prints and a group of fabrics containing adorable white-with-red stripes and dots create the spinning pinwheels that give this quilt playful charm. This will become an heirloom that family members will love to display every holiday season—a delicious little quilt to make you smile every time you see it.

MATERIALS

Yardage is based on 42"-wide fabric.

¾ yard of dark red fabric for outer border

⅝ yard *total* of assorted red fabrics for Pinwheel blocks

⅝ yard *total* of assorted white-with-red fabrics for Pinwheel blocks

½ yard of dark green fabric for setting triangles

½ yard of white-with-medium green fabric for half-square-triangle and alternate triangle blocks

¼ yard of medium green fabric for half-square-triangle and alternate triangle blocks

¼ yard of light green fabric for alternate triangle blocks

¼ yard of white-with-light green fabric for alternate triangle blocks

¼ yard of red-and-white stripe for inner border

½ yard of red stripe for binding

3 yards of fabric for backing

50" x 50" piece of batting

CUTTING

All measurements include ¼"-wide seam allowances. Cut all strips across the width of fabric (selvage to selvage).

From the assorted red fabrics, cut a total of:
5 strips, 3½" x 42"; crosscut into 50 squares, 3½" x 3½"

From the assorted white-with-red fabrics, cut a total of:
5 strips, 3½" x 42"; crosscut into 50 squares, 3½" x 3½"

From the medium green fabric, cut:
4 squares, 6" x 6"
1 square, 6¼" x 6¼"

From the white-with-medium green fabric, cut:
6 squares, 6" x 6"; cut *2 of the squares* once diagonally to yield 4 triangles
1 square, 6¼" x 6¼"

From the white-with-light green fabric, cut:
2 squares, 6" x 6"; cut each square once diagonally to yield 4 triangles
1 square, 6¼" x 6¼"

From the light green fabric, cut:
1 square, 6¼" x 6¼"

From the dark green fabric, cut:
4 squares, 8½" x 8½"; cut each square twice diagonally to yield 16 triangles
2 squares, 4½" x 4½"; cut each square once diagonally to yield 4 triangles

From the ¼ yard of red-and-white stripe, cut:
4 strips, 1½" x 42"

From the dark red fabric, cut:
5 strips, 4½" x 42"

From the ½ yard of red stripe, cut:
5 strips, 2½" x 42"

Peppermint Patties, designed and pieced by Mary Hickey, 45⅞" x 45⅞".
Machine quilted by Dawn Kelly.
Finished block: 5"

ASSEMBLING THE PINWHEEL BLOCKS

1. Using a pencil and your rotary-cutting ruler, draw a diagonal line from corner to corner on the wrong side of each 3½" white-with-red square. Place a marked square on each red square, right sides together. Stitch ¼" from both sides of the marked line. Cut the squares apart on the marked line. Press the seams toward the red. Make 100 half-square-triangle units. Trim the squares to 3" x 3".

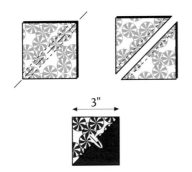

Make 100.

2. Arrange and sew four half-square-triangle units from step 1 as shown to make a Pinwheel block; press. Make 25 Pinwheel blocks.

Make 25.

ASSEMBLING THE HALF-SQUARE-TRIANGLE AND ALTERNATE BLOCKS

1. Place each medium green 6" square right sides together with a white-with-medium green 6" square. Using a pencil and your rotary-cutting ruler, draw a diagonal line from corner to corner on the wrong side of the white-with-medium green squares. Stitch ¼" from both sides of the line. Cut the squares apart on the marked line, flip open the squares, and press the seams toward the medium green. Make eight. Trim the blocks to 5½" x 5½".

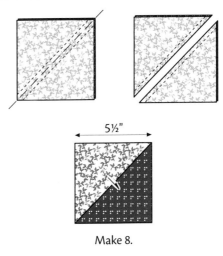

Make 8.

2. Repeating step 1, sew the white-with-medium green 6¼" square and the medium green 6¼" square together to make two half-square-triangle units; press the seams toward the medium green. Sew the light green 6¼" square and the white-with-light green 6¼" square together to make two half-square-triangle units; press the seams toward the light green.

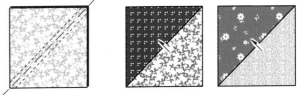

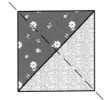
Make 2.

Make 2.

3. Cut the half-square-triangle units from step 2 in half diagonally as shown.

4. Sew a 6" triangle and a unit from step 3 together as shown. Make four blocks from each combination of fabrics. Trim the blocks to 5½" x 5½".

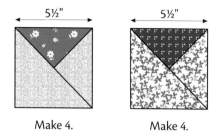

Make 4.   Make 4.

ASSEMBLING THE QUILT TOP

1. Refer to the assembly diagram to arrange the blocks and dark green 8½" side setting triangles into diagonal rows as shown.

2. Stitch the blocks and side triangles together in rows; press.

3. Stitch the rows together, adding the dark green 4½" corner triangles last. Press toward the corner setting triangles.

4. Refer to "Adding Borders" on page 17. Measure, cut, and sew the 1½"-wide striped inner-border strips and then the 4½"-wide dark red outer-border strips to the quilt top.

FINISHING THE QUILT

For detailed instructions on the following finishing techniques, refer to "Finishing Your Quilt" on page 18.

1. Cut and piece the backing fabric so that it is approximately 4" to 6" larger than the quilt top. Layer the quilt top with batting and backing. Baste the layers together.

2. Hand or machine quilt as desired. The quilt shown was machine quilted with a motif similar to peppermint patties.

3. Trim the batting and backing fabric so the edges are even with the quilt top. Add a hanging sleeve if desired.

4. Use the 2½"-wide red stripe strips to make the binding. Sew the binding to the quilt. Add a label to the quilt back.

Assembly diagram

CHRISTMAS STAR **WREATH**

T his gorgeous six-block quilt is filled with quilter's Christmas magic. We create the illusion of a circular wreath without ever sewing a curve and we make three different types of triangles without ever cutting a triangle. Although this enchanting block looks quite difficult, it is really rather simple and quite satisfying to make.

Christmas Star Wreath, designed by Mary Hickey, 45½" x 59".
Pieced by Pam Cope and machine quilted by Dawn Kelly.
Finished block: 11½"

MATERIALS

Yardage is based on 42"-wide fabric. Fat eighths measure 9" x 21".

1¼ yards of red floral fabric for outer border

⅝ yard of light green solid for sashing and inner border

⅝ yard *total* of assorted cream fabrics for block backgrounds

⅜ yard of dark green solid for cornerstones and middle border

1 fat eighth *each* of 3 dark red fabrics for blocks

1 fat eighth *each* of 3 light red fabrics for blocks

1 fat eighth *each* of 3 beige-and-red fabrics for block centers

1 fat eighth *each* of 3 dark green fabrics for blocks

1 fat eighth *each* of 3 light green fabrics for blocks

1 fat eighth *each* of 3 beige-and-green fabrics for block centers

½ yard of green stripe for binding

3⅛ yards of fabric for backing

50" x 63" piece of batting

CUTTING

All measurements include ¼"-wide seam allowances. Cut all strips across the width of fabric (selvage to selvage).

From the assorted cream fabrics, cut a *total* of:
4 strips, 3" x 42"; crosscut into 48 squares, 3" x 3"

3 strips, 1" x 42"; crosscut into 48 rectangles, 1" x 2½"

6 squares, 3¾" x 3¾"

From *each* of the dark red fabrics, cut:
2 squares, 3¾" x 3¾" (6 total)

4 squares, 3" x 3" (12 total)

From *each* of the light red fabrics, cut:
1 square, 3¾" x 3¾" (3 total)

4 squares, 2½" x 2½" (12 total)

From *each* of the beige-and-red fabrics, cut:
1 square, 7" x 7" (3 total)

From *each* of the dark green fabrics, cut:
2 squares, 3¾" x 3¾" (6 total)

4 squares, 3" x 3" (12 total)

From *each* of the light green fabrics, cut:
1 square, 3¾" x 3¾" (3 total)

4 squares, 2½" x 2½" (12 total)

From *each* of the beige-and-green fabrics, cut:
1 square, 7" x 7" (3 total)

From the light green solid, cut:
7 strips, 2½" x 42"; crosscut 3 *of the strips* into 7 rectangles, 2½" x 12"

From the dark green solid, cut:
4 strips, 1½" x 42"

2 squares, 2½" x 2½"

From the red floral fabric, cut:
5 strips, 7½" x 42"

From the green stripe, cut:
6 strips, 2½" x 42"

ASSEMBLING THE STAR WREATH BLOCKS

Each block is made using the pieces from one of the assorted cream fabrics for the background.

1. Using a pencil and your rotary-cutting ruler, draw a diagonal line from corner to corner on the wrong side of 24 cream 3" squares. Place a marked square on each 3" dark red square, right sides together. Stitch ¼" from both sides of the marked line. Cut the squares apart on the marked line. Press the seams toward the dark red. Make 24 sets of eight matching red half-square-triangle units. Repeat to make 24 sets of eight matching green half-square-triangle units, using the remaining marked cream squares and the 3" dark green squares. Trim the squares to 2½" x 2½".

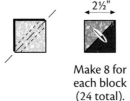

Make 8 for each block (24 total).　Make 8 for each block (24 total).

2. Stitch a 1" x 2½" cream rectangle to each of the half-square-triangle units from step 1 as shown. For each block, make four units (24 total) and four reversed units (24 total).

Make 4 and 4 reversed for each block.

3. Repeat step 1, drawing a diagonal line on the wrong side of each 3¾" cream square and each 3¾" light red square. Place a marked square on each 3¾" dark red square. Stitch and then cut the squares apart on the marked line. Press the seams toward the dark red. Make 12 sets of four matching red half-square-triangle units. Repeat to make 12 sets of four matching green half-square-triangle units, using the remaining marked cream squares and the 3¾" light green and dark green squares.

4. Cut each half-square-triangle unit from step 3 in half diagonally as shown. Match each cream/dark red unit with a light red/dark red unit to make an hourglass square as shown. Trim the blocks to 3" x 3". Make 12 sets of four matching red hourglass squares. Repeat to make 12 sets of four matching green hourglass squares.

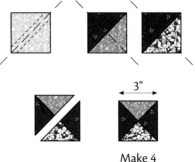

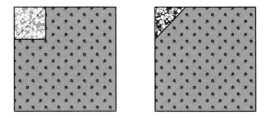

Make 4 for each block.

5. Draw a diagonal line from corner to corner on the wrong side of the 2½" light red squares. Place a marked square on each corner of a 7" beige-and-red square as shown, right sides together. Stitch along the marked lines. Trim ¼" from the stitching line. Flip open the triangle and press toward the light red. Make three red center units. Repeat to make three green center units, using the 2½" light green squares and the 7" beige-and-green squares.

Make 1 for each block.

6. Using the same combination of fabrics, arrange and sew the units from steps 2, 4, and 5 and four 3" cream squares together to make one block. Make three red blocks and three green blocks.

Make 3 red and
3 green blocks.

ASSEMBLING THE QUILT TOP

1. Stitch one 2½" x 12" light green sashing rectangle between two blocks as shown to make a block row. Make three rows.

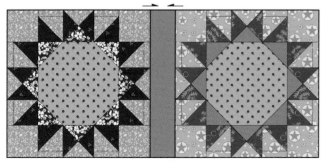

Make 3.

2. Stitch one 2½" dark green square between two 2½" x 12" light green sashing rectangles to make a sashing row. Make two rows.

Make 2.

3. Stitch the block rows and sashing rows together, alternating them as shown in the photo on page 46. Press the seams toward the sashing rows.

4. Refer to "Adding Borders" on page 17. Measure, cut, and sew the 2½"-wide light green solid inner-border strips, then the 1½"-wide dark green solid middle-border strips, and lastly the 7½"-wide red floral outer-border strips to the quilt top.

FINISHING THE QUILT

For detailed instructions on the following finishing techniques, refer to "Finishing Your Quilt" on page 18.

1. Cut and piece the backing fabric so that it is approximately 4" to 6" larger than the quilt top. Layer the quilt top with batting and backing. Baste the layers together.

2. Hand or machine quilt as desired. The quilt shown was machine quilted with a wreath motif in the blocks, leaves and branches in the light green sashing, and a floral swag in the outer border.

3. Trim the batting and backing fabric so the edges are even with the quilt top. Add a hanging sleeve if desired.

4. Use the 2½"-wide green stripe strips to make the binding. Sew the binding to the quilt. Add a label to the quilt back.

RIBBON **WREATH**

A single Star Wreath block forms the centerpiece of this little quilt. The same block design is presented here in a slightly larger size than the "Christmas Star Wreath" quilt on page 45. The exuberant scarlet ribbon and woven red border give this little quilt a bright future as a cherished Christmas heirloom.

MATERIALS

Yardage is based on 42"-wide fabric.

⅞ yard of white star fabric for background and borders

⅝ yard of medium green fabric for block and outer border

½ yard of light green fabric for block and binding

¼ yard of dark green fabric for block

½ yard of red fabric for woven border and appliqué

1 yard of fabric for backing

29" x 29" piece of batting

22 red buttons (optional)

CUTTING

All measurements include ¼"-wide seam allowances. Cut all strips across the width of fabric (selvage to selvage).

From the white star fabric, cut:

4 strips, 2" x 42"

5 strips, 1¼" x 42"; crosscut *1 of the strips* into 8 pieces, 1¼" x 2¾"

1 square, 8" x 8"

1 square, 4¼" x 4¼"

4 squares, 3½" x 3½"

4 squares, 3¼" x 3¼"

5 rectangles, 1½" x 8"

From the medium green fabric, cut:

4 strips, 3" x 42"

4 squares, 3¼" x 3¼"

From the light green fabric, cut:

3 strips, 2½" x 42"

1 square, 4¼" x 4¼"

4 squares, 2¾" x 2¾"

From the dark green fabric, cut:

2 squares, 4¼" x 4¼"

From the red fabric, cut:

6 rectangles, 2½" x 8"

ASSEMBLING THE STAR WREATH BLOCK

For detailed instructions and illustration on the following techniques, refer to "Assembling the Star Wreath Blocks" on page 48.

1. Draw a diagonal line on the wrong side of each 3¼" white star square. Place a marked square on each medium green square; stitch and then cut the squares apart. Press the seams toward the green. Make eight half-square-triangle units. Trim the squares to 2¾" x 2¾". Stitch a 1¼" x 2¾" white star rectangle to each half-square-triangle unit as shown in the diagram on page 48. Make four units and four reversed units.

2. Draw a diagonal line on the wrong side of the 4¼" white star square and the 4¼" light green square. Place a marked square on each dark green square; stitch and then cut the squares apart. Press. Cut each square in half diagonally. Match each white/dark green pair with a light green/dark green pair to make an hourglass square as shown in the diagram on page 48. Make four hourglass squares. Trim the squares to 3½" x 3½".

Ribbon Wreath, designed and pieced by Mary Hickey, 25½" x 25½".
Machine quilted by Dawn Kelly.
Finished block: 13½"

3. Draw a diagonal line on the wrong side of each 2¾" light green square. Place a marked square on each corner of the 8" white star square. Stitch and then trim away the excess fabric, leaving a ¼" seam allowance. Press toward the green. Make one center unit.

4. Arrange and sew the units from steps 1–3 and four 3½" white star squares together as shown to make the block.

Star Wreath block

5. Refer to "Appliqué Primer" on page 15 to make and apply the appliquéd bow, using the pattern on page 55. Refer to the quilt assembly diagram on page 54 and the photo on page 52 for placement as needed.

ADDING THE BORDERS

For detailed instructions, refer to "Adding Borders" on page 17.

1. Measure, cut, and sew the 1¼"-wide white star border strips to the center block.

2. To make the woven border, alternately sew the 2½" x 8" red rectangles and the 1½" x 8" white star rectangles together as

shown to make a strip set; press. Crosscut the strip set into four segments, 1½" wide.

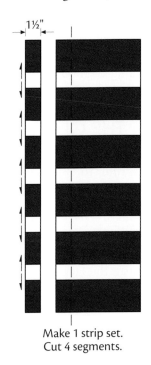

Make 1 strip set.
Cut 4 segments.

3. Center and sew a segment from step 2 to opposite sides of the quilt top. Trim the excess red fabric even with the edges of the quilt top; press toward the pieced border.

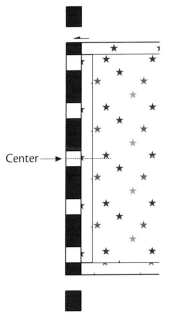

4. Stitch the remaining two segments from step 2 to the top and bottom edges of the quilt top; press.

5. Measure, cut, and sew the 2"-wide white star border strips to the quilt top and then the 3"-wide medium green outer-border strips to the quilt top.

FINISHING THE QUILT

For detailed instructions on the following finishing techniques, refer to "Finishing Your Quilt" on page 18.

1. Cut and piece the backing fabric so that it is approximately 4" to 6" larger than the quilt top. Layer the quilt top with batting and backing. Baste the layers together.

2. Hand or machine quilt as desired. The quilt shown was machine quilted with loops and stars in the background, arcs in the pieced block, outline stitching around the ribbon, and a lovely scroll design in the outer border.

3. Trim the batting and backing fabric so the edges are even with the quilt top. Add a hanging sleeve if desired.

4. Use the 2½"-wide light green strips to make the binding. Sew the binding to the quilt. Add the red buttons to the quilt front and a label to the quilt back as desired.

Assembly diagram

Enlarge patterns 125%.
Patterns do not include
seam allowances.

Cut 1 of each piece from red.

LITTLE FOREST

This magic little forest has trees with dots, checks, and even leaves, but the best trees have buttons. The trees will grow quickly using the folded-corner method. The Chain blocks are made up of speedy, simple four-patch units with a perky red square in the middle of each block. This quilt is fast and fun, and will be a joy for many years to come.

MATERIALS

Yardage is based on 42"-wide fabric.

⅞ yard of beige fabric for block backgrounds

⅞ yard of dark green fabric for outer border and binding

¼ yard of dark red fabric for inner border

¼ yard of medium green fabric for Chain blocks

⅛ yard *each* of 8 assorted green fabrics for Tree blocks

Scraps no smaller than 4" x 4" of 7 assorted red fabrics for Chain blocks

Scraps of assorted brown fabrics for Tree blocks

1⅓ yards of fabric for backing

31" x 43" piece of batting

Red star, heart, and round buttons (optional)

CUTTING

All measurements include ¼"-wide seam allowances. Cut all strips across the width of fabric (selvage to selvage).

From the beige fabric, cut:

2 strips, 2½" x 42"; crosscut into 28 squares, 2½" x 2½"

3 strips, 2¼" x 42"; crosscut into 48 squares, 2¼" x 2¼"

2 strips, 2¼" x 42"; crosscut into 16 rectangles, 1¾" x 2¼", and 16 rectangles, 1" x 2¼"

3 strips, 1½" x 42"

2 strips, 1¼" x 42"; crosscut into 16 rectangles, 1¼" x 3"

From *each* of the 8 assorted green fabrics, cut:

1 rectangle, 2¼" x 4" (8 total)

1 rectangle, 2¼" x 5½" (8 total)

1 rectangle, 2¼" x 6½" (8 total)

From the brown scraps, cut:

8 rectangles, 1¼" x 1½"

From the medium green fabric, cut:

3 strips, 1½" x 42"

From *each* of the red scraps, cut:

1 square, 2½" x 2½" (7 total)

From the dark red fabric, cut:

4 strips, 1½" x 42"

From the dark green fabric, cut:

4 strips, 3¾" x 42"

4 strips, 2½" x 42"

Little Forest, designed by Mary Hickey, 39" x 27".
Pieced by Judy Pollard and machine quilted by Dawn Kelly.
Finished block: 6"

ASSEMBLING THE TREE BLOCKS

1. Using a pencil and your rotary-cutting ruler, draw a diagonal line from corner to corner on the wrong side of each 2¼" beige square. Place a marked square on one end of each 2¼" x 4" green rectangle as shown. Stitch on the marked lines. Trim ¼" from the stitching line. Flip open the triangle and press the seam toward the green rectangle. Repeat on the opposite end of the green rectangle. Repeat to sew a marked square on each end of the 2¼" x 5½" and 2¼" x 6½" green rectangles as shown. Be sure to position the marked squares as shown on each unit. Keep each size of tree unit together.

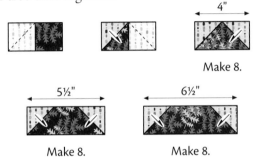

Make 8.

Make 8. Make 8.

2. Stitch one 4" tree unit from step 1 between two 1¾" x 2¼" beige rectangles as shown; press. Make eight.

3. Stitch one 5½" tree unit from step 1 between two 1" x 2¼" beige rectangles as shown; press. Make eight.

Make 8. Make 8.

4. Stitch one 1¼" x 1½" brown rectangle between two 1¼" x 3" beige rectangles as shown. Make eight trunk units.

Make 8.

5. Each Tree block is made from one green fabric. Arrange and sew one 6½" tree unit from step 1 and one unit from steps 2–4 together to make one Tree block. Repeat to make eight Tree blocks.

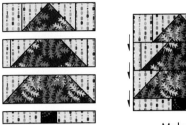

Make 8.

ASSEMBLING THE CHAIN BLOCKS

1. Stitch a 1½" x 42" beige strip to one long side of each 1½" x 42" medium green strip to make a strip set. Make three. Crosscut the strip sets into 56 segments, 1½" wide.

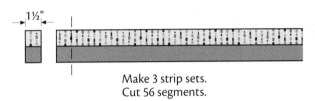

Make 3 strip sets.
Cut 56 segments.

2. Stitch two segments together as shown to make a four-patch unit. Make 28.

Make 28

3. Sew one 2½" red square between two 2½" beige squares; press. Make seven.

Make 7.

4. Stitch four units from step 2, one unit from step 3, and two 2½" beige squares together as shown to make one block. Make seven Chain blocks.

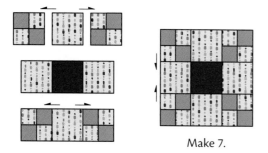

Make 7.

ASSEMBLING THE QUILT TOP

1. Refer to the quilt assembly diagram to arrange the blocks in three rows of five blocks each, alternating the Tree and Chain blocks in each row and from row to row as shown.

2. Stitch the blocks in each row together; press toward the Chain blocks. Stitch the rows together; press the seams in one direction.

3. Refer to "Adding Borders" on page 17. Measure, cut, and sew the 1½"-wide red inner-border strips and then the 3¾"-wide green outer-border strips to the quilt top.

FINISHING THE QUILT

For detailed instructions on the following finishing techniques, refer to "Finishing Your Quilt" on page 18.

1. Cut and piece the backing fabric so that it is approximately 4" to 6" larger than the quilt top. Layer the quilt top with batting and backing. Baste the layers together.

2. Hand or machine quilt as desired. The quilt shown was machine quilted with branches in the blocks, windy swirls in the background, and arcs in the borders.

3. Trim the batting and backing fabric so the edges are even with the quilt top. Add a hanging sleeve if desired.

4. Use the 2½"-wide dark green strips to make the binding. Sew the binding to the quilt. Stitch buttons to the trees as desired and add a label to the quilt back.

Assembly diagram

tiny blue cabins are set in a woodland village where the elves work in Santa's toy shop getting ready for the big day. Use the folded-corner method to make the trees and the roofs of the cabins. The rest of the cabin is pieced using the clever little template on page 66. This quilt has both a child-like appeal and a wonderful, sophisticated graphic effect.

Santa's Village, designed by Mary Hickey, 43" x 43".
Pieced by Joan Dawson and machine quilted by Dawn Kelly.
Finished block: 6"

MATERIALS

Yardage is based on 42"-wide fabric. Fat eighths measure 9" x 21".

2 yards of white fabric for block background and sashing

⅝ yard of medium green fabric for outer border

½ yard *total* or scraps of assorted green fabrics for Tree blocks

½ yard *total* or 1 fat eighth *each* of 6 assorted blue fabrics for Cabin blocks

⅜ yard *total* or 1 fat eighth *each* of 6 assorted red fabrics for Cabin blocks

¼ yard of dark red fabric for inner border

⅛ yard of yellow fabric for Cabin blocks and cornerstones

1 fat eighth of brown fabric for Tree blocks

½ yard of dark green fabric for binding

3 yards of fabric for backing

48" x 48" piece of batting

CUTTING

All measurements include ¼"-wide seam allowances. Cut all strips across the width of fabric (selvage to selvage).

From the white fabric, cut:
3 strips, 3½" x 42"; crosscut into 24 squares, 3½" x 3½", and 24 rectangles, 1" x 3½"

5 strips, 2¼" x 42"; crosscut into 72 squares, 2¼" x 2¼"

3 strips, 2¼" x 42"; crosscut into 24 rectangles, 1¾" x 2¼", and 24 rectangles, 1" x 2¼"

3 strips, 1¾" x 42"; crosscut into 6 strips, 1¾" x 20"

10 strips, 1½" x 42"; crosscut into 60 rectangles, 1½" x 6½"

2 strips, 3" x 20"

1 square, 6½" x 6½"

From the assorted green fabrics, cut a *total* of:
12 rectangles, 2¼" x 4"

12 rectangles, 2¼" x 5½"

12 rectangles, 2¼" x 6½"

From the brown fabric, cut:
1 strip, 1½" x 20"

From *each* of the assorted red fabrics, cut:
2 rectangles, 3½" x 6½" (12 total)

2 rectangles, 1½" x 2½" (12 total)

From *each* of the assorted blue fabrics, cut:
1 strip, 1¾" x 20" (6 total)

2 rectangles, 1½" x 2" (12 total)

2 squares, 1½" x 1½" (12 total)

4 rectangles, 1" x 3½" (24 total)

2 rectangles, 1" x 1½" (12 total)

From the yellow fabric, cut:
2 strips, 1½" x 42"; crosscut into 48 squares, 1½" x 1½"

From the dark red fabric, cut:
4 strips, 1½" x 42"

From the medium green fabric, cut:
5 strips, 3¼" x 42"

From the dark green fabric, cut:
5 strips, 2½" x 42"

ASSEMBLING THE TREE BLOCKS

1. Using a pencil and your rotary-cutting ruler, draw a diagonal line from corner to corner on the wrong side of each 2¼" white square. Place a marked square on one end of each of the 2¼" x 4" green rectangles as shown. Stitch on the marked lines. Trim ¼" from the stitching line. Press the seams toward the green rectangles. Repeat on the opposite end of the green rectangles. Repeat to sew a marked square on each end of the 2¼" x 5½" and 2¼" x 6½" green rectangles as shown. Be sure to position the marked squares as shown on each unit. Keep each size of tree units together.

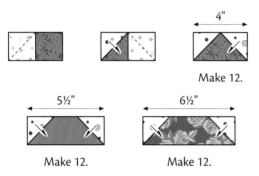

Make 12.

 Make 12.   Make 12.

2. Stitch a 4" tree unit from step 1 between two 1¾" x 2¼" white rectangles as shown; press. Stitch a 5½" tree unit from step 1 between two 1" x 2¼" white rectangles as shown; press.

Make 12.   Make 12.

3. Sew the 1½" x 20" brown strip between two 3" x 20" white strips as shown; press. Crosscut the strip set into 12 segments, 1¼" wide.

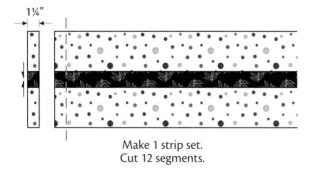

1¼"

Make 1 strip set.
Cut 12 segments.

4. Arrange and sew one 6½" tree unit from step 1, one 4" tree unit and one 5½" tree unit from step 2, and one segment from step 3 together as shown to make one block. Repeat to make 12 Tree blocks.

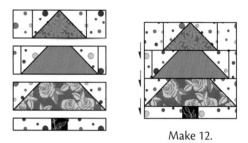

Make 12.

ASSEMBLING THE CABIN BLOCKS

1. Using a pencil and your rotary-cutting ruler, draw a diagonal line from corner to corner on the wrong side of each 3½" white square. Place a marked square on one end of each of the 3½" x 6½" red rectangles as shown. Stitch on the marked lines. Trim ¼" from the stitching line; press the seams toward the red rectangles. Repeat on the opposite end of the red rectangle, positioning the marked squares as shown. Make 12 roof units.

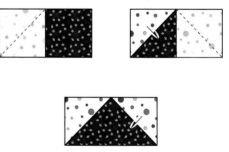

Make 12.

2. Stitch a 1¾" x 20" white strip to one long side of each 1¾" x 20" blue strip to make a strip set; press. Make six strip sets. Using template A on page 66, position the template with the angled line exactly on the seam line of the strip set. From each strip set, cut two pieces with the shaded side of the template on top of the blue strip. Then flip the template

over, repositioning it as before, and cut two reversed pieces. (Don't worry that the grain line will be on the partial bias when stitched into the Cabin blocks.) Cut a total of 12 units and 12 reversed units.

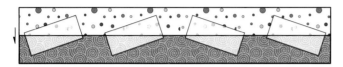

Make 6 strip sets.

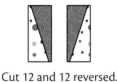

Cut 12 and 12 reversed.

3. To make the door section, sew one 1½" blue square and one 1½" x 2½" red rectangle together as shown; press. Make 12.

Make 12.

4. To make the window section, sew one 1" x 1½" blue rectangle, one 1½" yellow square, and one 1½" x 2" blue rectangle together as shown; press. Make 12.

Make 12.

5. Each block is made using the pieces from one of the assorted blue fabrics for the cabin. Arrange one unit from steps 1–4, two 1" x 3½" blue rectangles, and two 1" x 3½" white rectangles as shown. Stitch the cabin

pieces together in a horizontal row. The cabin unit should measure 3½" x 6½". Stitch the cabin unit and roof unit together to complete one block. Repeat to make 12 Cabin blocks.

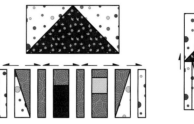

Make 12.

ASSEMBLING THE QUILT TOP

1. Refer to the assembly diagram on page 66 and the photo on page 62 to arrange the blocks and the 6½" white square in five rows of five blocks each, alternating and rotating the Tree blocks and Cabin blocks in each row and from row to row as shown.

2. To make the block rows, stitch a 1½" x 6½" white rectangle between each block and at the beginning and end of each row as shown; press.

Make 5.

3. To make the sashing rows, stitch five 1½" x 6½" white rectangles and six yellow squares together as shown; press. Make six rows.

Make 6.

4. Refer to the assembly diagram to stitch the sashing and block rows together as shown. Press the seams toward the sashing rows.

5. Refer to "Adding Borders" on page 17. Measure, cut, and sew the 1½"-wide red inner-border strips and then the 3¼"-wide green outer-border strips to the quilt top.

FINISHING THE QUILT

For detailed instructions on the following finishing techniques, refer to "Finishing Your Quilt" on page 18.

1. Cut and piece the backing fabric so that it is approximately 4" to 6" larger than the quilt top. Layer the quilt top with batting and backing. Baste the layers together.

2. Hand or machine quilt as desired. The quilt shown was machine quilted with swirls and outlines in the blocks, and leaves and branches in the borders.

3. Trim the batting and backing fabric so the edges are even with the quilt top. Add a hanging sleeve if desired.

4. Use the 2½"-wide dark green strips to make the binding. Sew the binding to the quilt. Add a label to the quilt back.

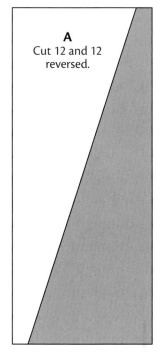

A
Cut 12 and 12 reversed.

Assembly diagram

TOYLAND **TABLE RUNNER**

The cabins and trees from "Santa's Village" on page 61 do double duty by providing the blocks for this adorable table runner. I had great fun hunting for and finding candy-themed fabrics. You could do the same by looking for toy, animal, pinecone, or any Christmas-themed print. With the folded-corner method, the roofs of the cabins and the trees will grow quickly from your sewing machine, and you'll have fun piecing the rest of the little Cabin blocks.

Toyland Table Runner, designed and pieced by Mary Hickey, 14½" x 70".
Machine quilted by Dawn Kelly.
Finished block: 6"

MATERIALS

Yardage is based on 42"-wide fabric. Fat eighths measure 9" x 21".

⅞ yard of dark red fabric for Cabin blocks, borders, and binding

⅝ yard of red-and-white fabric for outer border

½ yard of green plaid for sashing and inner border

½ yard of white fabric for block backgrounds

⅛ yard *each* of 3 assorted green fabrics for Tree blocks

1 fat eighth of dark green stripe for Cabin blocks

1 fat eighth of brown fabric for Tree blocks

Scraps of red-and-white stripe fabric for windows and doors

1¼ yards of fabric for backing

19" x 74" piece of batting

2 small red tassels (optional)

CUTTING

All measurements include ¼"-wide seam allowances. Cut all strips across the width of fabric (selvage to selvage).

From the white fabric, cut:

1 strip, 3½" x 42"; crosscut into 4 squares, 3½" x 3½", and 4 rectangles, 1" x 3½"

2 strips, 2¼" x 42"; crosscut into 24 squares, 2¼" x 2¼"

1 strip, 2¼" x 42"; crosscut into 8 rectangles, 1¾" x 2¼", and 8 rectangles, 1" x 2¼"

1 strip, 1¾" x 20"

2 strips, 3" x 8"

From the assorted green fabrics, cut a *total* of:

4 rectangles, 2¼" x 4"

4 rectangles, 2¼" x 5½"

4 rectangles, 2¼" x 6½"

From the brown fabric, cut:

1 strip, 1½" x 8"

From the dark green stripe, cut:

2 rectangles, 3½" x 6½"

From the dark red fabric, cut:

5 strips, 2½" x 42"

8 strips, 1" x 42"; crosscut *2 of the strips* into 2 strips, 1" x 15", and 4 strips, 1" x 11"

1 strip, 1¾" x 20"

2 rectangles, 1½" x 2"

2 squares, 1½" x 1½"

4 rectangles, 1" x 3½"

2 rectangles, 1" x 1½"

From the red-and-white stripe scraps, cut:

2 squares, 1½" x 1½"

2 rectangles, 1½" x 2½"

From the green plaid, cut:

3 strips, 2" x 42"

1 strip, 2½" x 42"; crosscut into 6 rectangles, 2½" x 6½"

1 square, 6½" x 6½"

From the red-and-white fabric, cut:

3 strips, 2¼" x 42"

1 square, 10" x 10"; cut in half diagonally to yield 2 triangles

ASSEMBLING THE TREE BLOCKS

For detailed instructions and illustration on the following techniques, refer to "Assembling the Tree Blocks" on page 64.

1. To make the 4" tree units, sew a 2¼" white square on each end of the 2¼" x 4" green rectangles. To make the 5½" tree units, sew a 2¼" white square on each end of the 2¼" x 5½" green rectangles. To make the 6½" tree units, sew a 2¼" white square on each end of the 2¼" x 6½" green rectangles. Make four of each unit.

2. Stitch a 1¾" x 2¼" white rectangle on each side of the 4" tree unit. Stitch a 1" x 2¼" white rectangle on each side of the 5½" tree unit. Make four of each unit.

3. Sew the 1½" x 8" brown strip between two 3" x 8" white strips. Crosscut four segments, 1¼" wide, to make four trunk units.

4. Stitch one of each tree unit and one trunk segment together to make a block as shown. Make four Tree blocks.

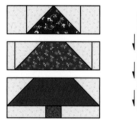
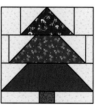

Make 4.

ASSEMBLING THE CABIN BLOCKS

For detailed instructions and illustration on the following techniques, refer to "Assembling the Cabin Blocks" on page 64.

1. To make the roof units, stitch a 3½" white square to each end of a 3½" x 6½" dark green stripe rectangle. Make two roof units.

2. Stitch the 1¾" x 20" white strip and red strip together along the long sides. Using template A on page 66, cut two units and two reversed units.

3. To make the door unit, stitch a 1½" red square and a 1½" x 2½" red stripe rectangle together. Make two door units.

4. To make the window unit, stitch a 1" x 1½" red rectangle, a 1½" red stripe square, and a 1½" x 2" red rectangle together. Make two window units.

5. Arrange one unit from steps 1–4, two 1" x 3½" red rectangles, and two 1" x 3½" white rectangles as shown. Stitch the cabin pieces together in a horizontal row. Then stitch the cabin unit and roof unit together to complete the block. Make two Cabin blocks.

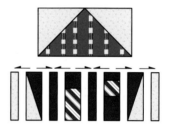

Make 2.

ASSEMBLING THE RUNNER

1. Arrange the blocks, six 2½" x 6½" green plaid rectangles, and the 6½" green plaid square in one row as shown. Stitch the pieces together and press.

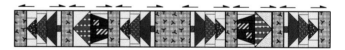

2. Refer to "Adding Borders" on page 17 to piece three 2"-wide green plaid strips together. From the pieced strip, cut two strips to fit the length of the block row and stitch them to each of the long sides.

3. Repeat step 2 to measure, cut, and sew the 1"-wide red strips, then the 2¼"-wide red-and-white strips, and lastly the remaining 1"-wide red strips.

4. Stitch one 1" x 15" red strip to each end of the quilt top; press.

5. Sew a 1" x 11" red strip to both shorter sides of each 10" red-and-white triangle and trim as shown below. Sew a triangle to each end of the quilt top as shown in the assembly diagram; press.

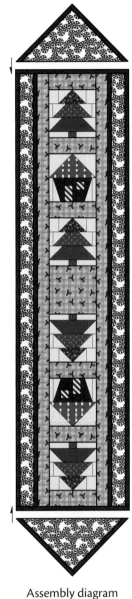

Assembly diagram

FINISHING THE RUNNER

For detailed instructions on the following finishing techniques, refer to "Finishing Your Quilt" on page 18.

1. Cut and piece the backing fabric so that it is approximately 4" to 6" larger than the quilt top. Layer the quilt top with batting and backing. Baste the layers together.

2. Hand or machine quilt as desired. The quilt shown was machine quilted with branches in the trees, in-the-ditch quilting in the cabins, holly leaves in the green sashing and border, squiggles in the red border, and a wonderfully cute curly design in the red-and-white border and triangles.

3. Trim the batting and backing fabric so the edges are even with the quilt top.

4. Use the 2½"-wide dark red strips to make the binding. Sew the binding to the quilt. Hand stitch a tassel to each end, if desired, and add a label to the quilt back.

THE GREAT KINDERGARTEN ANGEL CHRISTMAS PAGEANT

Faces gleaming and smiles beaming, these little kindergartners are dressed in their best clothes, socks almost matched, faces scrubbed, wings pinned to their backs, and hearts and stars held in their hands as they march down the aisle in the darkened auditorium for their Great Kindergarten Christmas Pageant. These angels are appliquéd with a fusible web followed by a straight-stitch outline around all the pieces and a few hand stitches around their little cheeks and chins. Get out your smallest scraps for their tiny shoes and socks and dresses, and plan for great fun as you outfit them and add their sweet little smiles.

MATERIALS

Yardage is based on 42"-wide fabric.

1 yard of dark blue dot fabric for blocks and outer border

1 yard of light blue fabric for appliqué block backgrounds

⅝ yard of tan fabric for appliqué block backgrounds

¼ yard of red-and-white stripe for inner border

¼ yard of white facing fabric for wings and angel faces

Scraps of peach, tan, white, red, green, blue, brown, and "blonde" fabrics for appliquéd angels

½ yard of navy blue fabric for binding

2⅝ yards of fabric for backing*

42" x 42" piece of batting

1 yard of lightweight fusible web

Navy blue thread

Water-soluble pen

.01 black permanent pen

If backing fabric is 42" wide after washing, you can use a single width of 1⅓ yards.

CUTTING

All measurements include ¼"-wide seam allowances. Cut all strips across the width of fabric (selvage to selvage).

From the dark blue dot fabric, cut:

4 strips, 3" x 42"

1 strip, 3" x 42"; crosscut into 4 squares, 3" x 3", and 8 rectangles, 1¾" x 3"

4 strips, 1¾" x 42"

From the tan fabric, cut:

2 strips, 3" x 42"; crosscut into 16 squares, 3" x 3"

2 strips, 1¾" x 42"

4 squares, 8" x 8"

From the light blue fabric, cut:

2 strips, 4¼" x 42"; crosscut into 4 rectangles, 4¼" x 8", and 4 squares, 4¼" x 4¼"

2 strips, 3" x 42"; crosscut into 16 rectangles, 1¾" x 3", and 8 squares, 3" x 3"

2 strips, 1¾" x 42"

1 square, 8" x 8"

From the red-and-white stripe, cut:

4 strips, 1½" x 42"

From the navy fabric, cut:

5 strips, 2½" x 42"

The Great Kindergarten Angel Christmas Pageant, designed and pieced by Mary Hickey, 37½" x 37½".
Machine quilted by Dawn Kelly.
Finished block: 7½"

ASSEMBLING APPLIQUÉ BLOCK BACKGROUNDS

1. Sew a 1¾" x 42" dark blue strip to one long side of a 1¾" x 42" tan strip to make a strip set; press. Make two.

Make 2.

2. Sew a 1¾" x 42" dark blue strip to one long side of a 1¾" x 42" light blue strip to make a strip set; press. Make two.

Make 2.

3. Place a strip set from step 1 on top of a strip set from step 2, right sides together, with the tan fabric on top of the dark blue fabric. Crosscut a total of 32 segment pairs, 1¾" wide.

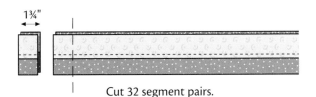

1¾"

Cut 32 segment pairs.

4. Stitch the segment pairs together to make a four-patch unit. Make 32 four-patch units.

Make 32.

5. Sew one 3" tan square between two four-patch units as shown; press. Make 12.

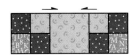

Make 12.

6. Sew one 8" tan square between two units from step 5 as shown; press. Make four. Set the remaining units from step 5 aside for step 4 of "Assembling the Quilt Top."

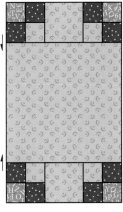

Make 4.

7. Sew one 3" light blue square between two four-patch units as shown; press. Make four.

Make 4.

8. Sew the 8" light blue square between two units from step 7 as shown; press. Set the remaining units from step 7 aside for step 6 of "Assembling the Quilt Top."

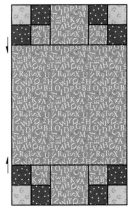

Make 1.

APPLIQUÉING THE ANGEL BLOCKS

Refer to "Appliqué Primer" on page 15 to make the appliqué shapes, using the patterns on pages 78–82, and for detailed instructions on each appliqué method.

1. Using the face-and-turn method on page 15, layer a piece of facing fabric and the chosen wing or angel face fabric right sides together. Using a water-soluble pen, trace and then cut out the shapes, adding ¼" around the edges for seam allowance.

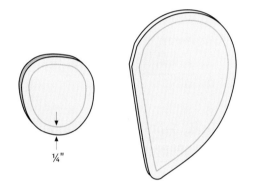

2. Using a tiny stitch, sew along the marked lines. Leave one side of the wings and the top of the heads open as shown. Trim the sewn edges to ¹⁄₁₆", leaving the ¼" seam allowance along the open edges.

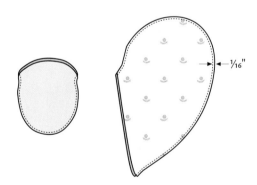

3. Spray each piece with water to remove the marked line. Turn each shape right side out and press thoroughly. Use a permanent pen to draw the facial details on each face.

4. Using the fusible-web method on page 15, prepare the hair and clothing shapes for each angel. Roughly cut out each shape and fuse to the chosen fabric. Cut out each shape on the drawn line.

5. Refer to the quilt assembly diagram on page 77 and the photo on page 74 for placement as needed. Position all the pieces for one angel on one background unit from either step 6 or 8 of "Assembling Appliqué Block Backgrounds." Pin the face and wings in place. Remove the hair and clothing pieces. Machine stitch the raw edges of the heads and wings to the block as shown.

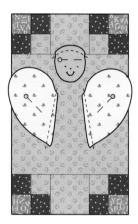

6. Reposition the hair and clothing pieces on the background unit. Start with piece 1 and add the remaining pieces in numerical order. Fuse the pieces in place. Use navy blue thread to topstitch around the edges of all the pieces except the bottom of the face and the outside edges of the wings. You may want to stitch around a piece two or three times to create contrast or to smooth out the stitching line.

ASSEMBLING THE QUILT TOP

1. Sew one 1¾" x 3" dark blue rectangle between two 1¾" x 3" light blue rectangles. Press toward the light blue. Make eight units.

2. Sew one 3" dark blue square between two 3" light blue squares. Press toward the light blue. Make two units.

3. Sew one 3" dark blue square between two 3" tan squares. Press toward the tan. Make two units.

4. To make row A, arrange and sew two units from step 1, two units from step 5 of "Assembling Appliqué Block Backgrounds," two 4¼" light blue squares, and one 4¼" x 8" light blue rectangle as shown; press. Make two rows.

5. To make row B, arrange and sew two units from step 1, one unit from step 2, and two tan appliquéd angel blocks; press. Make two rows. Pin the angel wings as shown.

6. To make row C, arrange and sew two units from step 3, two 4¼" x 8" light blue rectangles, two units from step 7 of "Assembling Appliqué Block Backgrounds," and the light blue appliquéd angel block; press. Make one row.

7. Sew rows A, B, and C together as shown in the assembly diagram; press. Use matching thread to hand stitch the bottom of the chins and tack the wings to the quilt top with five or six stitches.

8. Refer to "Adding Borders" on page 17. Measure, cut, and sew the 1½"-wide striped inner-border strips and then the 3"-wide dark blue outer-border strips to the quilt top.

Assembly diagram

FINISHING THE QUILT

For detailed instructions on the following finishing techniques, refer to "Finishing Your Quilt" on page 18.

1. Cut and piece the backing fabric so that it is approximately 4" to 6" larger than the quilt top. Layer the quilt top with batting and backing. Baste the layers together.

2. Hand or machine quilt as desired. The quilt shown was machine quilted with feathery swirls in the backgrounds of the angels, arcs and ovals in the outer blocks, and a heart-and-star vine in the outer border.

3. Trim the batting and backing fabric so the edges are even with the quilt top.

4. Use the 2½"-wide navy strips to make the binding. Sew the binding to the quilt. Add a label to the quilt back.

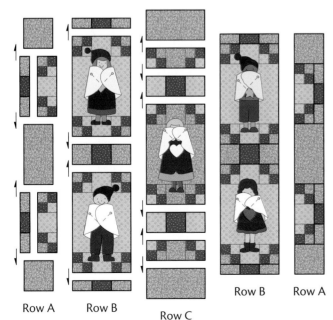

Row A   Row B   Row C   Row B   Row A

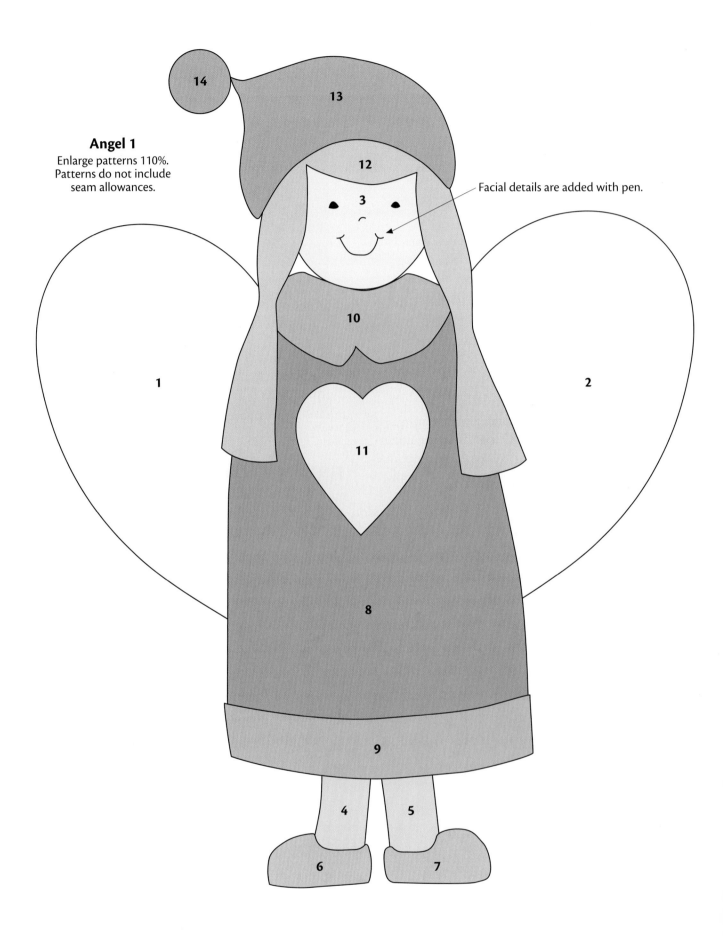

Angel 1
Enlarge patterns 110%.
Patterns do not include
seam allowances.

Facial details are added with pen.

Angel 2
Enlarge patterns 110%.
Patterns do not include
seam allowances.

Facial details are added with pen.

Angel 3
Enlarge patterns 110%.
Patterns do not include
seam allowances.

Facial details are added with pen.

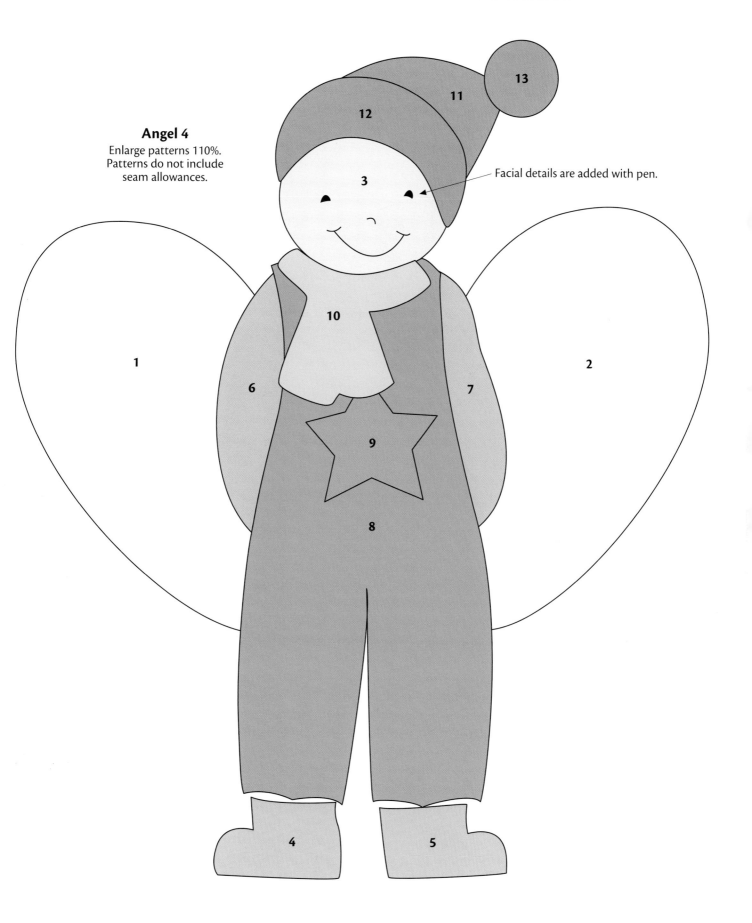

Angel 4
Enlarge patterns 110%.
Patterns do not include
seam allowances.

Facial details are added with pen.

Angel 5
Enlarge patterns 110%.
Patterns do not include
seam allowances.

Facial details are added with pen.

MIDNIGHT **STAR**

Warm reds, delicate greens, and soft hues of beige create a soothing wash of color in this lovely quilt made of two different pieced blocks. The beige bands in the double Snowball blocks link with the beige backgrounds between the star points to create a graceful wash of color and the interesting illusion of a diagonal square, transparent and soothing. Each block is constructed entirely of simple folded corners. The addition of simple little nine patches in five of the Star blocks creates interest and energy in this gentle Christmas wall hanging.

Midnight Star, designed by Mary Hickey, 41½" x 41½".
Pieced by Mary Hickey and Pat Blodgett, and machine quilted by Dawn Kelly.
Finished block: 6"

MATERIALS

Yardage is based on 42"-wide fabric.

1⅜ yards of red floral fabric for outer border

1 yard *total* of assorted beige fabrics for Star blocks and Double Snowball blocks

⅓ yard of medium green stripe for Star blocks and inner border

¼ yard of mottled green fabric for Double Snowball blocks

¼ yard *each* of 3 assorted light green fabrics for Double Snowball blocks

⅛ yard *each* of 2 assorted medium green fabrics for Star blocks

¼ yard *each* of 4 assorted small-scale red fabrics for Star blocks

⅛ yard *total* or scraps no smaller than 4" x 8" of 4 assorted large-scale red fabrics for Star blocks

½ yard of dark red fabric for binding

2⅞ yards of fabric for backing

45" x 45" piece of batting

CUTTING

All measurements include ¼"-wide seam allowances. Cut all strips across the width of fabric (selvage to selvage) unless instructed otherwise.

From *each* of the 4 assorted small-scale red fabrics, cut:

3 strips (12 total), 2" x 21"; crosscut into 104 squares, 2" x 2"

1 rectangle, 1½" x 10" (4 total)

2 rectangles, 1½" x 5" (8 total)

From the assorted beige fabrics, cut a *total* of:

5 strips, 3½" x 42"; crosscut into 48 squares, 3½" x 3½"

5 strips, 2" x 42"; crosscut into 52 rectangles, 2" x 3½"

8 rectangles, 1½" x 10"

4 rectangles, 1½" x 5"

From *each* of the 4 assorted large-scale red fabrics, cut:

2 squares, 3½" x 3½" (8 total)

From *each* of the 2 medium green fabrics, cut:

1 strip (2 total), 2" x 42"; crosscut into 40 squares, 2" x 2"

From the medium green stripe, cut:

4 strips, 1½" x 42"

12 squares, 2" x 2"

From *each* of the 3 assorted light green fabrics, cut:

4 squares, 6½" x 6½" (12 total)

From the mottled green fabric, cut:

3 strips, 2" x 42"; crosscut into 48 squares, 2" x 2"

From the *lengthwise grain* of the red floral fabric, cut:

4 strips, 5" x 44"

From the dark red fabric, cut:

5 strips, 2½" x 42"

MAKING THE STAR BLOCKS

1. Using a pencil and your rotary-cutting ruler, draw a diagonal line from corner to corner on the wrong side of each 2" red square. Align a marked square on one end of each 2" x 3½" beige rectangle, right sides together. Stitch on the marked line. Trim ¼" from the stitching line. Flip the red triangle up and press toward the square. Repeat on the opposite end of the beige rectangle, positioning the matching marked square as shown. Make four matching units for each block (52 total).

Make 52.

2. Sew matching 1½" x 10" beige rectangles to both long sides of a 1½" x 10" assorted red rectangle to make strip set A. Make one strip set from each red (four total). Cut a total of 10 segments, 1½" wide.

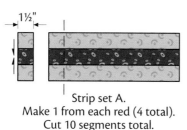

Strip set A.
Make 1 from each red (4 total).
Cut 10 segments total.

3. Using the same combination of fabrics that you used for the A strip sets, sew a 1½" x 5" assorted red rectangle to both long sides of a 1½" x 5" beige rectangle to make strip set B. Make one strip set from each red (four total). Cut a total of five segments, 1½" wide.

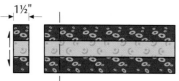

Strip set B.
Make 1 from each red (4 total).
Cut 5 segments total.

4. Using A and B segments from the same combination of fabrics, arrange two strip set A segments and one strip set B segment as shown. Sew the segments together to make a nine-patch unit. Make five.

Make 5.

5. Arrange and sew four matching units from step 1, four matching 2" medium green squares, and either a 3½" assorted red square *or* a nine-patch unit from step 4 together as shown to make a block. Make the number of blocks indicated for each combination.

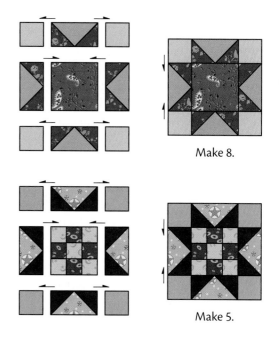

Make 8.

Make 5.

MAKING THE DOUBLE SNOWBALL BLOCKS

1. Using a pencil and your rotary-cutting ruler, draw a diagonal line from corner to corner on the wrong side of each 3½" beige square. With right sides together, place a marked square on opposite corners of each 6½" light green square as shown. Stitch on the marked line. Trim ¼" from the stitching line. Flip open the triangles on the large square and press toward the beige triangles. Repeat for

the remaining corners of each square, positioning the marked squares as shown. Make 12.

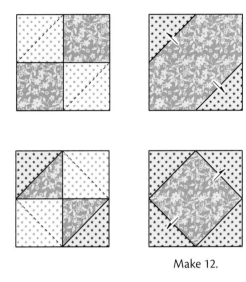

Make 12.

2. Draw a diagonal line from corner to corner on the wrong side of each 2" mottled green square. Place a marked square on each corner of the squares from step 1. Stitch on the marked lines. Trim ¼" from the stitching line. Flip open the triangles and press the seams toward the green triangles to complete one Double Snowball block. Make 12 blocks.

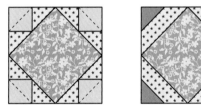

Make 12.

MARY'S HELPFUL HINT: MATCHING POINTS

To create the soft, washed effect of this quilt, take care to match the point where the beige print of the Double Snowball block meets the beige print of the Star blocks. Pin the points where the blocks need to match, and then sew them together using a large basting stitch. If the points match nicely, sew them with a regular stitch size. If they don't match, refer to "Rapid Ripping" on page 12 to help you rip them out, and then stitch them again.

ASSEMBLING THE QUILT TOP

1. Refer to the photo on page 84 to arrange the blocks into five horizontal rows of five blocks each, alternating the Star and Double Snowball blocks in each row and from row to row as shown.

2. Sew the blocks in each row together; press the seams toward the Double Snowball blocks. Sew the rows together, pressing the seams all in one direction.

3. Refer to "Adding Borders" on page 17. Measure, cut, and sew the 1½"-wide green stripe inner-border strips and then the 5"-wide red floral outer-border strips to the quilt top.

FINISHING THE QUILT

For detailed instructions on the following finishing techniques, refer to "Finishing Your Quilt" on page 18.

1. Cut and piece the backing fabric so that it is approximately 4" to 6" larger than the quilt top. Layer the quilt top with batting and backing. Baste the layers together.

2. Hand or machine quilt as desired. The quilt shown was machine quilted with a small medallion in the centers of the Double Snowball blocks, curving lines and in-the-ditch quilting in the Star blocks, and a beautiful swirl design in the borders.

3. Trim the batting and backing fabric so the edges are even with the quilt top.

4. Use the 2½"-wide dark red strips to make the binding. Sew the binding to the quilt. Add a label to the quilt back.

WATCHING FOR SANTA

We are fortunate to have many wonderful conversation prints available. Sometimes it's hard to think of a way to use them to their best advantage. A quilt like "Watching for Santa" gives you a wonderful opportunity to show them off. By using folded corners you can avoid having to make set-in seams or mitered corners. The black print sashing adds more depth to the illusion of space created by the "windows." However, nothing can give you the illusion that these adorable puppies and kittens have any attention span whatsoever.

MATERIALS

Yardage is based on 42"-wide fabric.

1 yard of novelty fabric for Attic Windows blocks*

⅝ yard of black fabric for sashing and inner border

⅜ yard of dark green fabric for outer border

⅜ yard *total* or scraps no smaller than 3" x 9" of assorted green fabrics for blocks

⅜ yard *total* or scraps no smaller than 3" x 7" of assorted red fabrics for blocks

¾ yard of red-with-white stars fabric for outer border and binding

1½ yards of fabric for backing

39" x 45" piece of batting

*If you don't plan to fussy cut the motifs, you will need only ½ yard. If you plan to fussy cut, you may need to purchase extra fabric, depending on how many 4½" motifs you can cut from it. See page 12 for more information on fussy cutting.

CUTTING

All measurements include ¼"-wide seam allowances. Cut all strips across the width of fabric (selvage to selvage).

From the novelty fabric, cut:
20 squares, 4½" x 4½"

From the assorted green fabrics, cut a *total* of:
20 rectangles, 2" x 4½"
20 squares, 2" x 2"

From the assorted red fabrics, cut a *total* of:
20 rectangles, 2" x 6"

From the black fabric, cut:
11 strips, 1½" x 42"; crosscut *3 of the strips* into 15 rectangles, 1½" x 6"

From the dark green fabric, cut:
2 strips, 4½" x 42"
1 square, 4½" x 4½"

From the red-with-white stars fabric, cut:
2 strips, 4½" x 42"
5 strips, 2½" x 42"
1 square, 4½" x 4½"

ASSEMBLING THE BLOCKS

1. Stitch a 2" x 4½" green rectangle to each 4½" novelty square as shown; press.

Make 20.

2. Using a pencil and your rotary-cutting ruler, draw a diagonal line from corner to corner on the wrong side of each 2" green square. With right sides together, place a marked square on each 2" x 6" red rectangle as shown. Stitch on the marked line. Trim ¼" from the stitching line. Flip open the square and press toward the green triangle.

Make 20.

3. Arrange matching units from steps 1 and 2 as shown. Stitch the units together to make one block; press. Make 20 blocks.

Make 20.

Watching for Santa, designed by Carolann Palmer, 35½" x 42".
Pieced by Cleo Nollette and machine quilted by Dawn Kelly.
Finished block: 5½"

ASSEMBLING THE QUILT TOP

1. Refer to the photo on page 90 to arrange and sew together three 1½" x 6" black sashing rectangles and four blocks, alternating them as shown to make a block row; press. Make five rows.

Make 5.

2. Measure the length of all the block rows. If they differ, calculate the average and consider this the length. Trim four 1½"-wide black strips to fit that measurement.

3. Stitch the block rows and the black sashing strips from step 2 together, alternating them as shown in the photo.

ADDING THE BORDERS

For detailed instructions, refer to "Adding Borders" on page 17.

1. Measure, cut, and sew the 1½"-wide black inner-border strips to the quilt top.

2. Measure, cut, and sew a 4½"-wide dark green outer-border strip to the right side and a 4½"-wide red star border strip to the left side of the quilt top.

3. Measure the quilt through the center from side to side and cut the remaining 4½"-wide green strip and 4½"-wide red strip to fit that measurement.

4. Draw a diagonal line from corner to corner on the wrong side of the 4½" red square and the 4½" green square. With right sides together, place a marked red square on one end of the trimmed green strip from step 3 as shown. Stitch on the marked line. Trim ¼" from the stitching line. Flip open the square

and press toward the red triangle. Repeat to stitch the marked green square to the trimmed red strip from step 3.

Make 1.

Make 1.

5. Sew the green outer-border strip from step 4 to the top edge and the red outer-border strip from step 4 to the bottom edge of the quilt top as shown in the photo on page 90.

FINISHING THE QUILT

For detailed instructions on the following finishing techniques, refer to "Finishing Your Quilt" on page 18.

1. Cut and piece the backing fabric so that it is approximately 4" to 6" larger than the quilt top. Layer the quilt top with batting and backing. Baste the layers together.

2. Hand or machine quilt as desired. The quilt shown was machine quilted with straight lines, stars, and lightbulbs.

3. Trim the batting and backing fabric so the edges are even with the quilt top.

4. Use the 2½"-wide red-with-white stars strips to make the binding. Sew the binding to the quilt. Add a label to the quilt back.

FROLICKING **FROSTIES**

These happy snowmen are having a great time frolicking in the winter frost. The trees in their forest have quite an attitude. All the big, rounded shapes make them easy to appliqué. I used a permanent pen to draw the snowmen's eyes and smiles, and then stitched tiny buttons to create the coal on the fronts of their tubby tummies. The plaid sashing and binding adds a lot of pizzazz to this already energetic little bunch.

MATERIALS

Yardage is based on 42"-wide fabric.

1 yard of gray dot fabric for background

¾ yard of red checked fabric for sashing, inner border, and binding

¾ yard of dark red fabric for outer border

⅓ yard of white for snowmen appliqués

Scraps of assorted green, gold, red, brown, navy blue, and black fabrics for clothing, trees, and star appliqués

1¾ yards of fabric for backing

33" x 56" piece of batting

7 tiny black buttons

.01 black permanent pen

CUTTING

All measurements include ¼"-wide seam allowances. Cut all strips across the width of fabric (selvage to selvage).

From the gray dot fabric, cut:
1 rectangle, 12¼" x 19½"
6 squares, 9½" x 9½"

From the red checked fabric, cut:
5 strips, 2½" x 42"
6 strips, 1½" x 42"; crosscut *1 of the strips* into 3 rectangles, 1½" x 9½"

From the dark red fabric, cut:
5 strips, 4¼" x 42"

APPLIQUÉ THE BLOCKS

1. Refer to "Appliqué Primer" on page 15 to make the snowmen, tree, and star appliqué shapes, using the patterns on pages 96–102 and the desired appliqué method. Apply the shapes to the gray dot background squares and rectangle. Refer to the assembly diagram on page 95 and the photo on page 94 for placement.

2. Using your favorite appliqué method, hand or machine stitch the pieces to the appropriate block background. The pattern pieces are numbered in the order they should be appliquéd.

3. Use a permanent pen to draw the faces on the snowmen. Sew buttons on two of the snowmen as shown in the photo.

Frolicking Frosties, designed by Mary Hickey, 51¾" x 29".
Appliquéd by Joyce Zivojnovich and machine quilted by Dawn Kelly.
Finished blocks: 6 blocks, 9" x 9", and 1 block, 11¾" x 19"

ASSEMBLING THE QUILT TOP

1. Sew one 1½" x 9½" red-checked sashing rectangle between two 9½" blocks as shown in the assembly diagram. Make sure all the appliqué blocks are upright and not rotated sideways or upside down. Make three rows.

2. Measure the length of the three block rows. If they differ, calculate the average and consider this the length. From two of the 1½"-wide red checked strips, cut three sashing strips to fit that measurement.

3. Stitch the block rows, the 12¼" x 19½" appliqué block, and the three sashing strips from step 2 together, alternating them as shown in the assembly diagram.

4. Refer to "Adding Borders" on page 17. Measure, cut, and sew the remaining 1½"-wide red checked inner-border strips and then the 4¼"-wide dark red outer-border strips to the quilt top.

FINISHING THE QUILT

For detailed instructions on the following finishing techniques, refer to "Finishing Your Quilt" on page 18.

1. Cut and piece the backing fabric so that it is approximately 4" to 6" larger than the quilt top. Layer the quilt top with batting and backing. Baste the layers together.

2. Hand or machine quilt as desired. The quilt shown was machine quilted with swirls and outline quilting in the blocks, and a star and heart vine in the borders.

3. Trim the batting and backing fabric so the edges are even with the quilt top.

4. Use the 2½"-wide red checked strips to make the binding. Sew the binding to the quilt. Add a label to the quilt back.

Assembly diagram

Snowman 1
Enlarge patterns 125%.
Patterns do not include
seam allowances.

Facial details are added with pen.

Snowman 2
Enlarge patterns 125%.
Patterns do not include
seam allowances.

Facial details are added with pen.

Snowman 3
Enlarge patterns 125%.
Patterns do not include
seam allowances.

Facial details are added with pen.

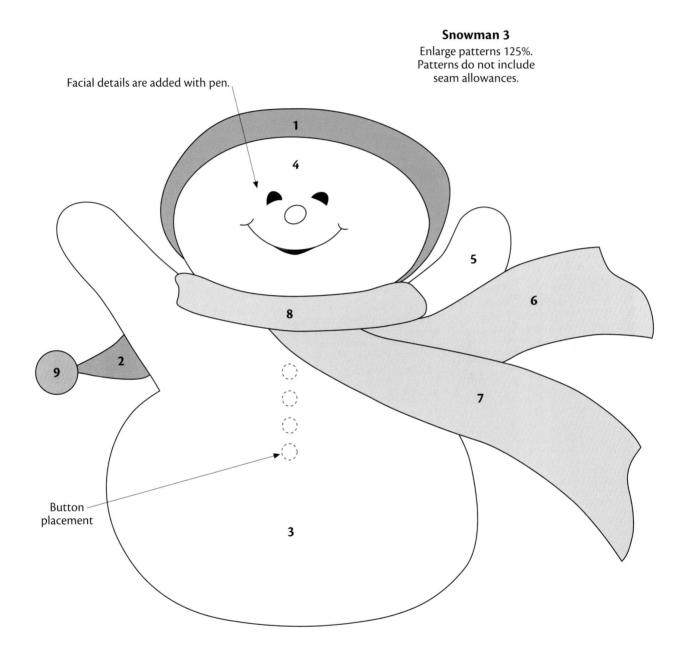

Button
placement

Snowman 4
Patterns are full sized. *Do not enlarge.*
Patterns do not include
seam allowances.

Facial details are added with pen.

Snowman 5
Enlarge patterns 125%.
Patterns do not include
seam allowances.

Facial details are added with pen.

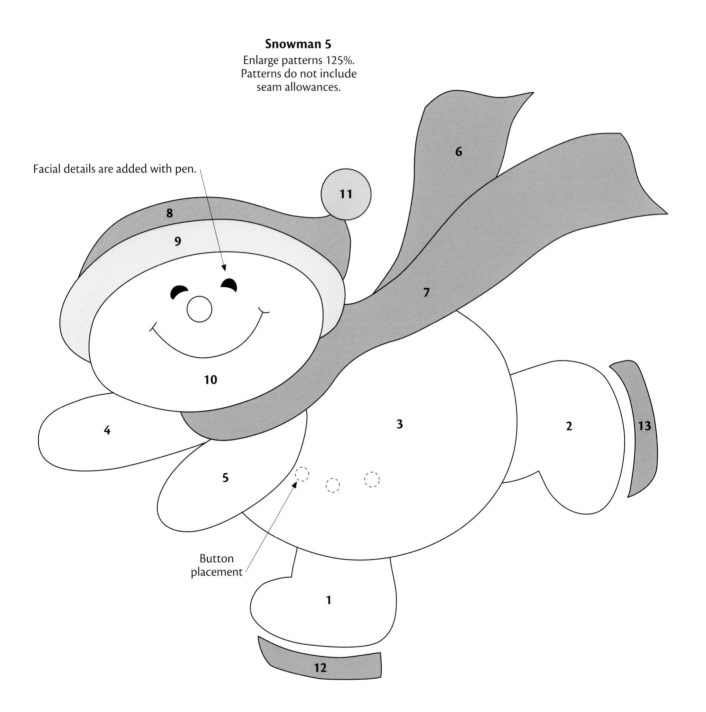

Button
placement

Snowman 6
Patterns are full sized. *Do not enlarge.*
Patterns do not include
seam allowances.

Facial details are added with pen.

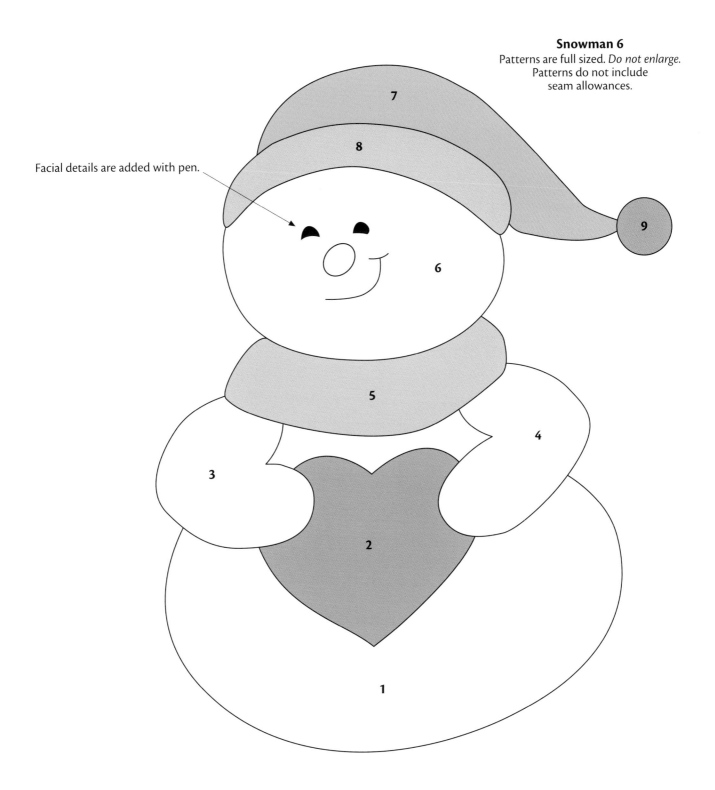

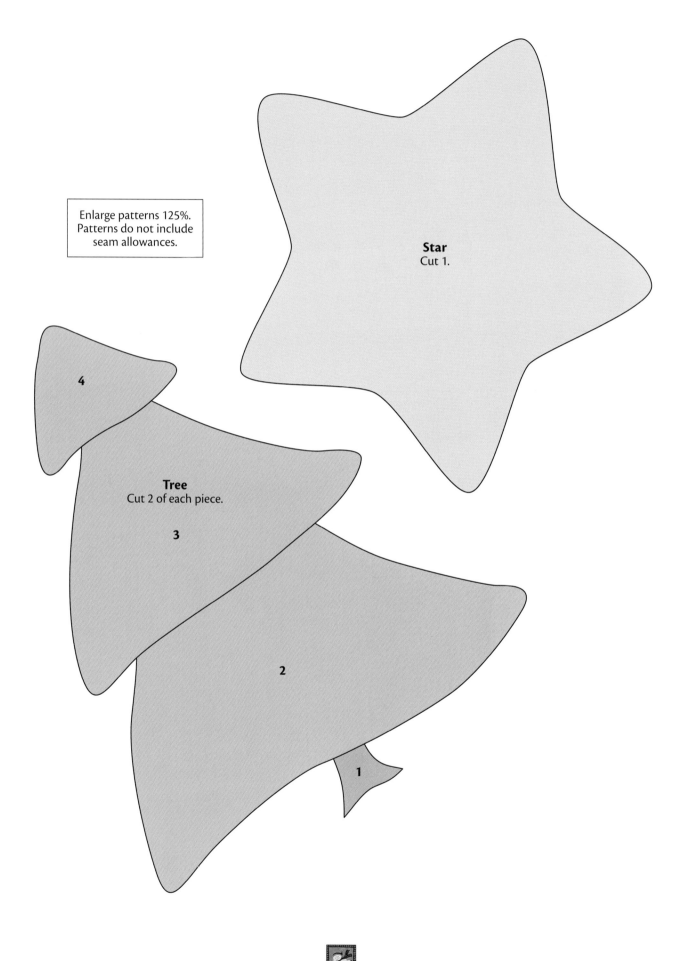

Enlarge patterns 125%.
Patterns do not include
seam allowances.

Star
Cut 1.

4

Tree
Cut 2 of each piece.

3

2

1

CHRISTMAS **SKI TRIP**

S wishing back and forth, zigzagging downhill on a sparkling winter day is a Christmas tradition among many families. This soft, cuddly flannel lap quilt is so easy you can make it in an afternoon. The blocks are simply two large triangles with a sashing strip between each row. Easy, big, and bold, this quilt is a Christmas sensation.

MATERIALS

Yardages are based on 42"-wide flannel fabrics.

1⅞ yards of dark red print for blocks, sashing, and middle border

1⅜ yards of black fabric for inner border, outer border, and binding

1 yard of light red print for blocks and sashing

1 yard of dark beige print for blocks and sashing

1 yard of light beige print for blocks and sashing

4 yards of fabric for backing

64" x 72" piece of batting

CUTTING

All measurements include ¼"-wide seam allowances. Cut all strips across the width of fabric (selvage to selvage).

From the light beige print, cut:

3 strips, 7" x 42"; crosscut into 15 squares, 7" x 7"

1 strip, 6½" x 42"; crosscut into 15 rectangles, 2½" x 6½"

From the light red print, cut:

3 strips, 7" x 42"; crosscut into 15 squares, 7" x 7"

1 strip, 6½" x 42"; crosscut into 10 rectangles, 2½" x 6½"

From the dark beige print, cut:

3 strips, 7" x 42"; crosscut into 12 squares, 7" x 7"

1 strip, 6½" x 42"; crosscut into 12 rectangles, 2½" x 6½"

From the dark red print, cut:

3 strips, 7" x 42"; crosscut into 12 squares, 7" x 7"

1 strip, 6½" x 42"; crosscut into 8 rectangles, 2½" x 6½"

7 strips, 4½" x 42"

From the black fabric, cut:

8 strips, 2½" x 42"

6 strips, 2" x 42"

7 strips, 1¾" x 42"

ASSEMBLING THE BLOCKS

1. Using a pencil and your rotary-cutting ruler, draw a diagonal line from corner to corner on the wrong side of each 7" light beige square. Place a marked square on each light red square, right sides together. Stitch ¼" from both sides of the marked line. Cut the squares apart on the marked line. Press the seams toward the red. Make 30 half-square-triangle units. Trim the squares to 6½" x 6½".

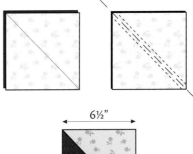

Make 30.

Christmas Ski Trip, designed and pieced by Mary Hickey, 60" x 68".
Machine quilted by Dawn Kelly.
Finished block: 6"

2. Repeat step 1, drawing a diagonal line on the wrong side of each 7" dark beige square. Place a marked square on each dark red square. Stitch and then cut the squares apart; press. Make 24 half-square-triangle units. Trim the squares to 6½" x 6½".

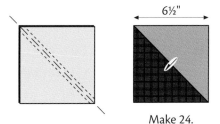

Make 24.

ASSEMBLING THE QUILT TOP

1. Refer to the assembly diagram to arrange six units from step 1 of "Assembling the Blocks," three 2½" x 6½" light beige rectangles, and two 2½" x 6½" light red rectangles, alternating them as shown. Sew the pieces together; press. Make five rows.

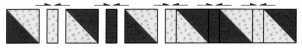

Make 5.

2. Arrange six units from step 2 of "Assembling the Blocks," three 2½" x 6½" dark beige rectangles, and two 2½" x 6½" dark red rectangles, alternating them as shown in the assembly diagram. Sew the pieces together; press. Make four rows.

3. Arrange and stitch the rows from steps 1 and 2 together, alternating them as shown in the assembly diagram.

4. To make borders with butted corners, refer to "Adding Borders" on page 17. Measure, cut, and sew the 2"-wide black inner-border strips, then the 4½"-wide dark red middle-border strips, and lastly the 1¾"-wide black outer-border strips to the quilt top.

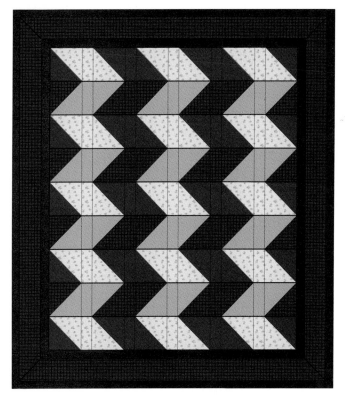

Assembly diagram

MITERED BORDERS

If you prefer to miter your border corners as I did, follow the steps below. You may need to cut additional strips to achieve the required length.

1. Join the 2"-wide black inner-border strips end to end to make a continuous strip. Then estimate the finished outside dimensions of your quilt top, including all the borders, and add 2" to 3" to this measurement. Cut four strips from the long strip to fit that measurement.

2. Repeat step 1 to join, measure, and cut the 4½"-wide dark red middle-border strips and the 1¾"-wide black outer-border strips. Note you may want to sew the individual border strips together along the long edge and treat the resulting unit as a single border strip.

3. Mark the centers of the quilt edges and border strips with pins.

4. Measure the length and width of the quilt top through the center in both directions. Place a pin at each end of the side border strips to indicate the length of the quilt top. Repeat with the top and bottom border strips.

5. Pin the side border strips to the quilt top, matching the pin marks at the centers and matching the pins at the ends of the border strips with the edges of the quilt top. Stitch, beginning and ending the stitching ¼" from the raw edges of the quilt top. Repeat with the top and bottom border strips. Press toward the border strips.

6. Lay one corner of the quilt top on the ironing board. Fold under one border strip at a 45° angle to the other strip. Press and pin.

7. Fold the quilt top, right sides together, and line up the edges of the border strips. Stitch along the pressed crease, sewing from the inner corner to the outer edge. Trim the seam allowance to ¼" and press the seam open. Miter the remaining corners in the same manner.

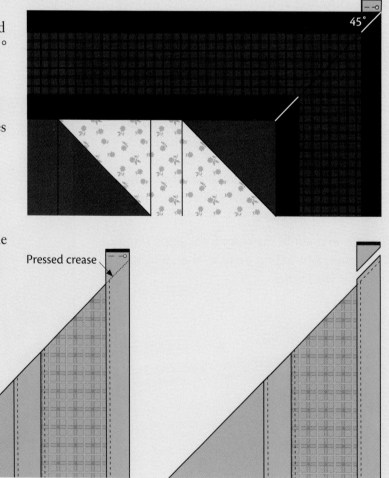

Pressed crease

FINISHING THE QUILT

For detailed instructions on the following finishing techniques, refer to "Finishing Your Quilt" on page 18.

1. Cut and piece the backing fabric so that it is approximately 4" to 6" larger than the quilt top. Layer the quilt top with batting and backing. Baste the layers together.

2. Hand or machine quilt as desired. The quilt shown was machine quilted with a vine design in the red blocks, a swirl design in the tan blocks, and a beautiful feathered vine design in the borders.

3. Trim the batting and backing fabric so the edges are even with the quilt top.

4. Use the 2½"-wide black strips to make the binding. Sew the binding to the quilt. Add a label to the quilt back.

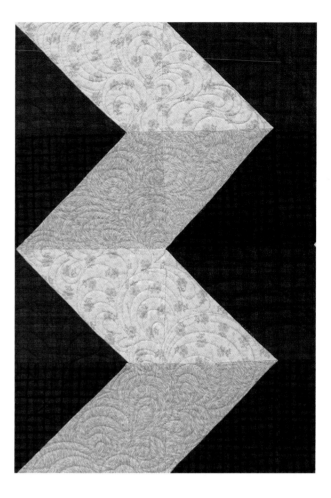